Anarchist Studies

VOLUME 14	2006	NUMBER 1

ADVERTISEMENTS   Email lw@l-w-bks.demon.co.uk

SUBSCRIPTIONS   2006 subscriptions are (for 2 issues):
Personal £20; Institutional £50.00;
Students £15

© 2006 Lawrence & Wishart
99a Wallis Road, London E9 5LN
Email: lw@l-w-bks.demon.co.uk
Tel: 020 8533 2506

ISSN 0967 3393

Text setting: E-Type
Cover illustration: *Big Idea* © Fly 2006

Anarchist Studies is indexed in Alternative Press Index, British Humanities
Index. C.I.R.A., Left Index, International Bibliography of the Social
Sciences, Sociological Abstracts and *Sonances*.

The cover of this issue, 'Big Idea' is by Fly, a New York based anarchist illustrator. Fly writes that she 'was born in a dumpster' (Canada). She finally landed in New York and has been squatting buildings in the Lower East Side of Manhattan since the late 1980s. Fly documents the comings and goings of the local community in paintings, illustrations and sometimes paints murals. She is a frequent contributor to *World War 3 Illustrated*, an anti-authoritarian publication based in New York. Fly has also self-published numerous comics & zines – a collection of these, CHRON!IC!RIOTS!PA!SM!, was published in 1998 by Autonomedia Press. A second book of 196 portraits and autobiographical stories, PEOPs, was published in 2003 by Soft Skull Press. Fly is currently bringing her squatted building 'up to code' so she will never be evicted again. www.bway.net/~fly

INTRODUCTION
Anarchism: Secularism, Religion and Diversity

This issue of *Anarchist Studies* concentrates on a paper by Sharif Gemie entitled 'The Trial of Fatima: Anarchists, Muslims and the *Monde Libertaire*, 2003-05'. Sharif's paper was written in October 2005, before the riots in the *banlieus*, and it takes issue with the position adopted by the French anarchist weekly on the recent law banning the display of 'ostentatious' religious symbols in French state schools. *Monde Libertaire* (ML), he argues, have wrongly considered that the law is well-directed, misled by their reliance on a crude and outmoded anarchist theory and a set of inherently sexist and racist assumptions, the latter having their roots in France's colonial past. Sharif's paper is of obvious interest to specialists in French affairs. But as I will suggest at the end of this piece, the issues that he raises have a broader significance, extending beyond French politics.

The discussion papers are with one exception supportive of Sharif's position. Neil McMaster develops the argument about French colonialism. Harold Barclay considers Sharif's treatment of Islam before turning to analyse the social exclusion of French Muslims and the recent riots. Georges Ubbiali lends some support to the idea of secularism in schools, but suggests that the cost of ML's defence of *laïcité* is an unacceptable neglect of the real issue in French politics: immigration. Beltràn Roça analyses ML's position as misguided commitment to outdated Enlightenment values. Whilst Paul Chambers broadens the discussion by attempting to tackle the relationship between anarchism, the state and religion more generally, Tom Cahill presents a personal reflection on the operation of the French law and its inconsistencies. The last paper in the collection is Ronald Creagh's. This presents a robust defence of ML and the principle of *laïcité*. In her concluding piece, L. Susan Brown reflects on these debates and presents a powerful plea for diversity, drawing on the experience of multiculturalism in Canada.

With the exception of L. Susan Brown, all the contributors are men. Both the consensus and the lack of gender balance reflect problems of communication and academic time rather than genuine agreement or lack of interest in the issue. Significantly more writers (from wide-range of backgrounds and disciplines) were invited to comment on Sharif's paper than had opportunity to respond. A copy was also sent to ML. Unfortunately, ML were unable or unwilling to reply (Ronald Creagh suggests some reasons why, but it is disappointing that the explanatory statement comes from him rather than ML's editor or editorial committee).

What are the main lines of the debate? There seems to be general agreement that France – not alone in Western Europe – is riven by racism, xenophobia and sexism; that minority immigrant populations are subject to discrimination, exclusion and oppression; that political elites have manipulated the 'headscarves affair' to suit their own agendas; that international politics has played an important role in the debate; and that the issue has forced strange new alliances between liberals, libertarians and their enemies, on both sides of the argument. There is an equally strong consensus that in non-Western societies Islam has adapted itself to openly patriarchal and deeply illiberal traditions and political regimes. Finally, all contributors agree that the decision whether or not to wear a headscarf should be considered a matter of individual choice and, assuming the choice is exercised freely, that its display might be determined by any number of different motivations. What is at issue in this debate is the symbolic significance of the headscarf in the public realm. Interpretations of its significance seem to map on to three interrelated arguments about the ('traditional') anarchist critique of religion, the treatment of the secular republican state's claims to neutrality and the legacy of French colonialism.

One view of religion is that anarchists are anti-clerical rather than anti-religious. From this point of view, the problem of religion lies in the institutional relationship of the church (or any other religious body) and the state. Religion itself does not present a problem for anarchists. As Harold Barclay argues, religious teachings can support a range of interesting and alternative institutional arrangements. Equally, as Paul Chambers and Beltràn Roca point out, religious movements can and have served as a vehicle for liberation. The alternative view is that anarchists reject the principle of religion. Rather than being opposed merely to its institutionalisation, they see in it a demand to submit to a superior will. This submission is said to lie at the root of all political authority, and it suggests that whilst churches and other religious institutions are parasitic on the state, religious faith importantly underpins it. This is a view usually associated with Bakunin but it has recently been revived by writers like Fredy Perlman who see in religion – Christianity in particular – a impulse to dominate nature (Mother Earth). A similar position informs Creagh's analysis.

On the second point, the state's claims to neutrality, the issue is how far the notion of a secular state – such as that modelled in France – is really a cover for the imposition of a set of bourgeois, Western and Euro-centric values. Critics of ML suggest that this is precisely the case. Indeed they are convinced that the republican model is less able than the liberal to uphold the liberties it claims to respect because it effectively excludes minority groups from public consideration. Ronald Creagh's response is that Anglo-Saxon writers – Tom Cahill happily includes himself in this category – are unable to grasp the concept of neutrality being defended. The secular state of course favours a particular set of class and non-class relations. But unlike the liberal state, which has dominated British and American political traditions, its aim is to maximize the liberty of citizens by confining questions of faith to a private realm. The secular republican state has no interest in accommodating the claims of competing social groups either by providing equal access to the state's resources or by recognising identities and claims to group memberships. Against writers like Beltràn Roca, who suggests that the state should take group claims and issues of identity seriously, Creagh argues that the liberal model provides no limit to toleration, that it encourages factionalism and, as a consequence, supports a permanent condition of social strife that benefits only the state.

The important corollary is that critics of ML argue that the secular state necessarily oppresses minorities and conclude that anarchists should seek to align themselves with all protest movements. From this perspective the campaign against the ban represents a challenge to the state's authority. Creagh contends that the ban on headscarves is simply not oppressive and that, whilst there are other good reasons why anarchists should make common cause with minorities (to fight racism, xenophobia, sexism and so forth) the freedom to display religious symbols in the public sphere is not one of them. From this point of view, it is wrongheaded to generalise the British experience of radical dissent and misguided to court alliances with groups who seek to reintroduce religion into the public realm.

Some of the arguments raised in this debate can be resolved. For example, it is possible to justify claims to identity using traditional rights theory (the argument would run something like: 'all individuals have a right to the membership of a particular cultural group'). Pace Roca, then, there is no reason to throw out 'Enlightenment' thinking in order to recognise diversity. And there may be good reasons to hang on to something like 'reason' or 'rationality' when it comes to arguments about creationism and intelligent design. Yet in general terms the positions represented by Sharif, on the one hand, and ML on the other, cannot easily be reconciled, certainly not in the combinations in which they are played out. After all, if religion is considered to be just another belief, which has the same status as a political interest, it is near impossible to treat the French government's (and ML's) fears seriously. By the same token, if one sincerely holds that religious faith falls into a different category of belief from, say, other political commitment, and that it necessarily implies submission and mystification, the suggestion that religious symbols (ignoring all the problems associated with 'ostentation') can be treated as marks of political protest is untenable.

The final issue, the legacy of French colonialism, is equally contentious. One of the main thrusts of Sharif's paper is that ML have misjudged the significance of the headscarf protest in France because they have been misled by a set of stereotypes inherited from the past. This point is developed in the paper by Neil McMaster. Rather than trying to discover why young French women have chosen to adopt the headscarf, ML have simply dismissed the wearers as victims of manipulation and patriarchal oppression. Mistakenly assuming that the headscarf indicates a commitment to (that fuzzy term) fundamentalism, they have also wrongly introduced into the debate a set of concerns about the toleration of other oppressive non-European practices. Georges Ubbiali contests this view, maintaining that the scarf is a symbol of female submission and that it should be resisted whatever the motives of the women who wear it. Creagh's response is rather different. He admits a tendency to sloppiness on behalf of some writers in the debate. It is important, he argues, not to presume that wearers of the headscarf are victims in any sense. Yet it is equally important that the demands of the groups who support these individuals are understood. It may be that in the current context the wearing of a headscarf is a sign of alienation, as much as deep religious commitment. Nonetheless, the protest has raised the profile of some rather dubious groups – some who want to take power in the state in order then to oppress the women they pretend to support. Moreover, if one is to avoid assumptions, Creagh argues that non-French must equally avoid reading too much into the legacy of colonialism and/or condemn those who endorse the ban as racists or Islamaphobes. The French cultural tradition of *laïcité* should also be respected.

Creagh's point about French culture is perhaps disingenuous, since it attempts to re-deploy multi-culturalist critiques against those who would level them against him. Nevertheless it usefully reveals the central tenet of the secular-republican case. Critics of ML suggest that anarchists should defend ideas of difference, diversity and pluralism. Whilst, as Beltràn Roca notes, anarchists want to stop short of relativism, these values are supported because they are important to libertarians and anarchists – not just because they help states to integrate minority populations (a somewhat contentious point and perhaps a red herring in the debate given the track record of institutional racism and civil rights abuses in liberal states). On Creagh's side it is of course possible to defend secularism as a cultural value. But it is not easy to do so without adopting a highly politicised notion of culture – one tied to a set of constitutional precepts that have their roots in France's revolutionary past. Creagh's argument – which is supported by a significant section of the French left – points to a homogeneous and static idea of Frenchness that sits uneasily with the principle of diversity traditionally associated with libertarian and anarchist politics. The issue posed by the headscarves debate, then, is not just one of religion, but the possibility of negotiating differences between diverse groups. The relevance of this issue extends far beyond ML's treatment of the scarf.

The contributions by Spencer Sunshine and Uri Gordon in this issue are not part of the discussion on Anarchism: Secularism, Religion and Diversity.

The Trial of Fatima: Anarchists, Muslims and the *Monde Libertaire*, 2003-05

SHARIF GEMIE

Fatima was the prophet Mohammed's daughter. In colonial Morocco, her name was used by French householders as a generic term for a female servant, in colonial Algeria it served to indicate a prostitute. Today, the same girl lives in France, and she is making the headlines. Recently she has appeared at two trials: it is the second of these which will be the subject of this article.

The first trial took place in late 2003 and early 2004, when Fatima was the subject of two major parliamentary enquiries, the first presided over by Jean-Louis Debré and second by Bernard Stasi. The stated brief of these bodies was to discuss the presence of religious symbols in public life but, as almost every French paper and commentator noted, their real subject was the presence of a few hundred veiled schoolgirls in French state schools. This is not a new issue: it first attracted public debate in the late 1980s. The Debré and Stasi committees produced two reports which, put together, were over a thousand pages long. These were then followed by 21 hours of parliamentary debate in February 2004, involving some 120 speakers. The final result of these deliberations was to change one word in the regulations governing the appearance of pupils in schools: prior to September 2004, school pupils were not allowed to show *ostentatoire* symbols of religious allegiance, after that date all *ostensible* symbols were banned. The difference between the two terms is hard to capture, even in French, but the first word could be translated as approximately equivalent to ostentatious, the second as noticeable or public.[1] The exact significance of this law is still being debated: while Sikh turbans and Jewish yarmulke are definitely banned, it is left to teachers and headteachers to decide whether a particular crucifix is *ostensible* or discreet. Even in the case of the veil, the law remains unclear. 'If I let my veil fall over my shoulders, they ban me', explained one schoolgirl to me, 'if I tie it behind my neck, and tell them it's a bandanna, they let me in.'

Polls indicated that the majority of French public opinion, and even the majority of French Muslim public opinion, were clearly in favour of this measure, but one qualification needs to be made to this point: debates were bitter and divisive. Many of France's most prestigious civil liberties and human rights organizations were critical of this legislation, and some elements within the teachers' trade unions opposed it. While the Greens were the only national party to refuse to support the legislation, it was an issue which split long-standing friends and allies. Even the libertarian left was divided. While, as will be seen, the *Monde Libertaire* mainly produced arguments solidly in favour of the law, other libertarian sources – such as the new web-site lmsi – were far more critical.[2]

Before moving onto our main subject, one brief word of explanation is needed concerning terminology. Amongst supporters of the legislation, the word *voile* (veil) was fairly consistently used to identify the *ostensible* symbol to which they objected. Among opponents, a wider range of terms of was used: *hijab, foulard* (headscarf) as well as *voile*. In many ways, *foulard* is probably the most accurate of these terms: these schoolgirls usually wore relatively loose bits of cloth that they draped over their heads. They did not follow Taliban-style strictness. If I was writing an anthropological essay concerning the schoolgirls' cultures, I would probably choose *foulard* as the most suitable word. However, as this paper principally concerns outsiders' perceptions, I will stick to the more commonly circulating term 'veil'.

THE *MONDE LIBERTAIRE*

So much for Fatima's first trial. Her second trial, which will form the main subject of this paper, took place in the columns of the *Monde Libertaire* (henceforth ML).

The ML began publishing in October 1954, as the voice of a newly reconstituted Fédération Anarchiste, but its origins can be traced back to *Le Libertaire* created by Sébastien Faure in December 1894. It is a weekly, which ceases publication for three months every summer. ML probably has a circulation of about ten thousand, making it arguably Europe's most widely read anarchist periodical. About five years ago it shifted from a largely black and white broadsheet format to its current, more colourful, twenty-four page tabloid format. At the same time, there was a shift from relatively long analytic articles to shorter, more polemical pieces. The ML remains the official voice of the Fédération Anarchiste (FA), a federation of several different currents of anarchist activism and critique. There are approximately eighty local groups within the FA, which also owns a well-equipped meeting-room and bookshop in Paris, and runs the prestigious Paris-based Radio libertaire.

Just as the FA is a federation, so the ML is not a rigidly-run mechanism for hammering out an agreed line. Indeed, there is a curious similarity between the structures of debates within the FA and those within Islamic culture: there is usually no acknowledged leader, but a series of experts who offer contrasting interpretations of a set of accepted principles, relying on their experience, their charisma or the force with which they argue to gain acceptance. (The formal hierarchy of Shi'a Islam in Iran, and its close involvement with state structures is atypical of Islam as a whole.) In practice, one finds that there are key issues on which the ML feels certain, and expects agreement from its readers (such as solidarity with workers' protests) and other issues on which disagreement and even confusion are usually acknowledged in a fairly mature and responsible manner. Often contributions appear from writers who are not FA members. One could cite the debates around the 2005 Euro-Constitution referendum as an example of the second approach: the ML published articles suggesting acceptance, rejection and abstention. Such a variety of opinions may well be appropriate. In areas where one sets neither the agenda nor the question, yes *and* no can sometimes be a proper response. Put simply, the main purpose of this paper is to suggest that the ML placed its discussions of the veil in the wrong category: its editors assumed that this was an area in which all ML-readers would agree, when it would have been more responsible to encourage debate and a plurality of opinions.

While writing this paper, it struck me how strange it was that one could now debate the ML *and* Islam, and that this issue had arisen in relation to the veil. Of course, no French paper has been able to ignore Muslim politics in recent years. The first issues of ML were published in the mid-1950s, during the Algerian War of Independence. The ML played a prominent part in publicizing the use of torture by the French army in Algeria, and also campaigned against the sending of conscripts to Algeria. But the FA always refused to support either the nationalist-revolutionary FLN (National Liberation Front) or the more Muslim MNA (Algerian National Movement), arguing that the war in Algeria was merely a battle between two bourgeoisies, French and Algerian, and that the proper anarchist attitude should be one of neutrality.[3] In more recent decades, discussions concerning Islam or French Muslims were relatively rare in the ML – until the war of the veil in 2003-04. This is rather curious: France has the largest Muslim population in Europe. Experts consider that between four to six million Muslims live in France: approximately one-tenth of France's population of 58 million. Nearly every estimate comes with the qualification that only about half of these are *practising* Muslims, but this point raises more questions about the status of the others. In many French towns, Muslim-Arabs, usually from North Africa, form a sub-proletariat: they are the street cleaners, the manual workers and the hotel maids. One of the few good cartoons raised by the topic of the veil came in the satirical weekly, the *Canard Enchaîné*. It showed an Arab construction worker, sweating over a heavy pneumatic drill, and grumbling 'And what about this drill? Does it constitute an *ostensible* sign of religious affiliation?' In a sense, ML is in a privileged position: with its circulation, its resources and its contacts, it has a unique opportunity to study, to analyse and to debate the re-constitution of a social hierarchy in a post-colonial country during globalization, and to develop a distinctively libertarian intervention on these important issues. The evidence of its coverage of the veil suggests that it has singularly failed to do this, and it is for this reason that it is worth considering this matter in more detail.

For this article, I have re-read twelve articles from May 2003 to October 2005, which – bearing in mind ML's three month summer holiday – amounts to one article every two months on average. Obviously, this is not an enormous corpus of material, but the arguments presented in these twelve articles are revealing. Without exception, they concern Islam in relation to French schools, to schoolgirls and to *laïcité*, the ideal of a secular public sphere. Significantly, the second and the fifth of these articles, which are probably the most hard-hitting of the twelve, are written by feminists in groups outside the FA. The widespread use of pseudonyms makes it difficult to identify the articles' authors with certainty, but three of the twelve papers seem to have been written by women, and none of them appear to have been written by authors with an Arab or Muslim name.

Only one of these articles is clearly against the proposed law of March 2004. A second article argues strongly against a dogmatic defence of *laïcité*, and a third suggests a type of neutrality on the issue. However, there can be no doubt about the ML's 'centre of gravity': the clear majority (nine) of the articles were clearly against the wearing of *le voile* in state schools. As the one anti-law article pointed out: there is a contradiction here. Anarchists pride themselves on their anti-authoritarian values. Why was France's leading anarchist weekly supporting the state's stigmatisation of a minority population?

During the course of 2003, the ML was presented with a new issue. Its contributors – many of them reasonably experienced political militants, some of them practised writers, none of them experts on Muslim culture – approached it awkwardly. Looking at these articles as a whole, it is clear that their first aim was to confirm an existing body of anarchist theory rather than to re-consider and to investigate – and one can hear the political gears crunching and screeching as they do so. Perhaps the most revealing line in all these articles is a single phrase concerning the writings by women in Bangladesh and Iran: they 'confirm what we know'.[4]

LAÏCITÉ

While these articles can be seen as being 'about Islam', this is not how the debate was presented to ML readers. Instead, the war of the veil was interpreted, firstly, as a debate for or against *laïcité*. Most ML contributors are deeply attached to this value. There is some reason for this: *laïcité* is a concept which has been developed, generation by generation, across over two centuries of French history. Often its progress is marked by clashes and crises: one could cite the now infamous Calas case of 1762-65, when the Enlightenment philosopher Voltaire rose to the defence of Jean Calas, a Protestant who suffered judicial torture and then execution after the false accusation that he had killed his own son to prevent his conversion to Catholicism. More relevant might be the Dreyfus Affair of 1895-1906, when a Jewish French army officer was wrongly accused of spying for Germany, and was sentenced to life imprisonment on Devil's Island. Anarchists were initially slow to respond. Bakunin and – more particularly – Proudhon had made some use of anti-semitic imagery in their writings, and there was an easy, sloppy assumption circulated among many anarchists that all Jews were rich bankers like Rothschild. It took a courageous minority of militants, headed by Sébastien Faure and Octave Mirbeau, to alert libertarians to the dangers of their toleration of anti-semitism. Mirbeau was particularly eloquent: he appealed for working-class support for Dreyfus.

> When injustice strikes a living being – even if he's your enemy – you get hit as well. By injustice, Humanity's split into two. You must heal it, ceaselessly, by your efforts and, if you're rebuffed, do it by force, if necessary. In defending him, who's been oppressed by every brutal force, by all the passions of a declining society, you're defending yourself in him, you're defending your people.[5]

From such cases there developed the ideal of a religiously neutral public sphere, open to all citizens, and free of prejudice and domination by any church or institution. For much of the late nineteenth century and early twentieth century, this ideal was enthusiastically supported by the labour movement, and secular schoolteachers often became socialist or communist militants. Among anarchists, a particularly militant strand of anti-clericalism developed, directed against the Church's influence in schooling and its frequent support for right-wing political causes.

An opinion poll showing that 65% of the French population supported the ideal of *laïcité* was therefore celebrated by ML: it demonstrated 'a most pleasing lucidity'. This was a simple, either/or choice. 'Either you believe in emancipation or you believe in submission', noted the author.[6] In another article on the hyper-provocative *Manifesto des indigènes de la République* [Manifesto of the Natives in the Republic] of April 2005, one contributor responded that this text should be rejected by ML readers as it was not an (acceptable) condemnation of colonialism but an (unacceptable) attack on *laïcité*.[7] One article made the necessary corrective: in practice, French *laïcité* has been largely created by authoritarian state action; it is based on an abstract ideal of the model citizen, stripped of all signs of personal identity, and who thus accepts the nation-state as the centre of their political universe.[8]

Like President Chirac himself, the writers for ML believed that their values of *laïcité* were being attacked by outsiders intent on destruction. ML drew back from spelling out the logical consequence of such attitudes – i.e. explicit support for the new law. In fact, this was even occasionally denied, but it remained the obvious lesson to be drawn by ML's readers.

THE VEIL

Like Chirac, Debré and Stasi, the ML spoke with great certainty about the meaning of the *voile*.

- 'The veil is a sign that the patriarchy that one believed was exhausted, has been revived in its most retrograde and virulent form: radical Islam.'[9]
- 'The veil is the symbol of a seclusion of women.'[10]
- '[The veil is] a direct attack on women, it is their negation.'[11]
- '[Choosing to wear a veil is] of course, the freedom to choose voluntary servitude.'[12]

There is an assumption of intellectual and political superiority in these phrases. Anybody who has studied this issue would concede that the *voile* is polysemic: it carries multiple meanings; it is context-sensitive. In Iran in the 1980s and in Afghanistan in the 1990s the actions taken by authoritarian Muslim groups to enforce the compulsory wearing of the veil are clear examples of a blatant disregard of women's autonomy. But to reduce the range of meanings of this millennia-old costume to these instances is absurd, and the insistence by these largely male, largely white, entirely non-Muslim commentators that they understand *the* meaning of the veil better than women who wear it really is an act of colossal political arrogance – surpassed only by Chirac's, Debré's and Stasi's pronouncements. None of the ML's writers make any effort to discuss the matter with any schoolchildren – let alone with the girls who wear the veils.[13] None of them attempt to understand the difficult situation faced by many girls in second-generation immigrant families, living 'an exile within an exile'.[14] Most surprising of all, ML contributors simply refuse to recognize the existence of an intense, exhausting, important, wide-ranging debate within French Muslims.[15] They ignore works such as the superb *L'une voilée, l'autre pas* [one veiled, the other not], a well-written, well-researched analysis of the issue by two French Muslim women who, making use of the techniques of participant-observation, consider as wide a spectrum of opinion and experience as is possible.[16] The controversial and iconoclastic Swiss-Muslim thinker Tariq Ramadam is simply hounded by ML's contributors; any defence of the veil or of Muslim identity is immediately and unthinkingly dismissed as simple fundamentalism.

Not one of these twelve articles is prepared to consider that a woman might freely choose to veil herself, or that – in certain contexts – veiling might even play a liberating role. None of them consider the obvious and frequent role of the veil as passport: a device which allows the transition of young Muslim women from conservative (but *not* fundamentalist) homes into modern schools. None of them notes the frequent apparent paradox of young women who arrive from North Africa, where they had never worn a veil, and then choose to wear a veil, for the first time, once they arrive in France. This practice suggests the role of the veil as a form of self-assertion, a way of saying that young Muslim women want integration into the French Republic *without* assimilation.

Instead, the veil becomes a blank sheet upon which ML's contributors rewrite a distinctly antique version of anarchist dogma. This argument is nicely demonstrated by the first point in a ten point programme concerning the *voile*.

1. The right to show one's body.[17]

I'd happily support such a right, 100%, but only if it was accompanied by the declaration of an equal and contrary right: the right to cover one's body. The significant point here is that while ML's contributors can see the necessity of the first right, the idea that the second right might also be appropriate simply does not apply. One reason for this attitude probably lies in an older anarchist aesthetic, in which 'the nude' is presented as symbolic of a kind of natural freedom, or a voice of truth and – conversely – the covering of the nude as a form of repression.[18] Once again, there is some validity in these ideas, but they clearly cannot be applied in this clumsy and ham-fisted manner.

Alongside this rather woolly aesthetic argument about bodily freedom, I can't help wondering if there's not a certain amount of good old-fashioned male lechery lurking in the columns of ML. On the one hand, ML does present an open platform for feminists and feminist arguments. On the other hand, reading through its issues one after another, it is impossible to ignore that almost every second issue contains a drawing or photo of a pretty young women wearing not many clothes. Do these images set the cultural and aesthetic standards by which the *voilées* are being judged?

A CONSPIRACY

Only one anti-law article asked readers to listen to the ideas of the *voilées*. The majority of articles clearly refused to do this, merely referring to them as 'manipulated' or as 'political pawns', mere teenagers who consciously or unconsciously were acting as agents for fundamentalists.[19] Referring to the sad case of the Turkish schoolgirl in Mulhouse who, in October 2004, shaved her head when her school refused to allow her entrance if she wore a veil, the ML commentator was contemptuous, considering that she spoke far too coherently to be genuine.[20] The master-minds behind this manipulation were often left anonymous, as is usually the case in such 'moral panics', but several ML writers point to the UOIF (the Union of French Islamic Organizations), which is referred to unproblematically as 'fundamentalist', with no discussion about what this confusing label might mean, and no evidence to explain why it was appropriate. Any activity by the UOIF in defence of *voilées* was immediately seen as manipulative and illegitimate by the majority of ML contributors. Once again, this was a strange argument: given the UOIF's open and explicit opposition to the new law, it would have been odd if they did not aid school-girls facing state repression. To date, all the evidence suggests that UOIF is acting entirely within the structures of the French law. What is still more strange is that the ML proposes no solidarity with the victims of state stigmatisation.

The same point led ML contributors to warn of the reality lurking behind this piece of cloth: behind the *voilées*, the fundamentalists and their violence against women, their sexual harassment of unveiled women in the housing estates, their polygamy, even their support for female genital mutilation – a familiar list of scare topics raised by every sundry Islamophobe across Europe, and which could have been cut-and-pasted from articles published in the right-wing *Figaro* or the trendy, soft-left *Libération*.[21] While each of these topics is profoundly serious, they simply are not relevant to the debate on the veil in France. If there are organized fundamentalist forces attempting to police the presence of women on French streets, then action should be taken against *those forces*, not against their victims. Male sexual violence deserves to be fought wherever it occurs – but, as yet, there is little convincing evidence that Muslim men are more likely to be violent than non-Muslims. As for female genital mutilation: this is little more than slander. There is no Qur'anic support for the practice whatsoever. In some African countries it existed as practice *before* Islam, and it has never been proposed by Muslim authorities although, to the shame of those same authorities, it has been tolerated. The countries with the worst records of female genital mutilation are not Muslim.

ISLAM

While the majority of these articles were hostile to what they termed fundamentalism, it is clear that this was part of a more general attitude. An article from May 2005 was explicit: it called on ML to

… fight Islam. This theme might make us uneasy because, after all, there are other people, some of them highly reprehensible, who speak of fighting Islam. But we know that our reasons for fighting Islam are not racism or the desire to replace one disease of the mind with another.[22]

This is interesting proposition. The ten thousand readers of the ML are being rallied to fight the world's two billion Muslims. And, above all, there are no qualifications to this call: it ignores both Islam's limited – but real – historical achievements and its potential to inspire aesthetic pleasure, scientific progress, social justice or human dignity. Muslim architecture, including the glories of the Alhambra in Granada, will have to be smashed. The delightful Arabo-Andalusian music, endlessly re-cycled in shaky videos by Moroccan television to aid elderly listeners with their afternoon siestas, will be banned. The Muslim scientific advances, which discovered algebra, identified alcohol and investigated alchemy, will be rejected by the new zealots of ML. Algerian *raï* music, unpopular with Muslim fundamentalists but still played by Muslim musicians, would also be forbidden. Under this new enlightened rule, we will even have to return to the Roman arithmetic, and ML will now bear the date MMVI, for the modern European system of counting, with its all-important use of the zero, was copied from Muslim mathematicians. Even the future of chess and draughts looks a bit dodgy.

It is hard to know what is saddest in this situation. Can one imagine Voltaire crying 'Fight Protestantism!' during the Calas Case? Or Faure and Mirbeau calling on anarchists to 'Fight Judaism!' during the Dreyfus Affair? The writers of ML are suffering from a deep and pronounced intellectual exhaustion. One gets the impression that they would only feel some understanding of the *voilées* if the schoolgirls justified their choices by citing passages from Proudhon (which would not be completely impossible). The most basic points to be derived from religious sociology escape ML's writers. Is it not blindingly obvious that a minority religion *deserves* a different treatment from that accorded to a majority religion, and that the civil liberties and respect given to minorities shape the real freedom enjoyed by the majority? Secondly, is it not also obvious than the development of new forms of Muslim faith are *symptoms* of other, deeper issues, rather than *causes* of problems? When Marx noted that religion is 'the cry of the heart in a heartless world' he was doing nothing less than calling for this type of sensitivity to the cultural and social role of religions. Lastly, it should never be forgotten that one impulse within Islam was an attempt to create a non-hierarchical religion. Of course, in practice this has largely failed, but this point alone should be enough to make anarchists interested in Islam.[23]

Another way to make the same point is to ask that the ML consider Muslims not Islam; that they address themselves to the real experience of real people living in France and not draw nightmare comparisons from the quite different contexts of Iran or Bangladesh. There is no one single Islam: instead, within the structures of cultural globalization, with its 'diasporic public spheres', new forms of Islam are being devised to express some of the resentments and aspirations of the first post-colonial generation from the families of Arab migrants.[24] In a context in which American hegemony is being justified through the use of crude anti-Islamic slogans, in which the European far right is exploiting anti-Muslim sentiment and in which European governments are policing travel and migration with ever-increasing severity,[25] the first duty of anarchists is that of solidarity with the victims of this repressive wave and *not* half-embarrassed expressions of support for state repression.

CONCLUSION: ONE SIZE FITS ALL?

ML's articles explicitly refer back to the universalism of the Enlightenment. Its contributors are against 'l'ethno-différencialisme'[26] and for universalism. But the ML is proposing a very peculiar form of universalism: a form which is based on uniquely French concepts of *laïcité*, a form which accepts western concepts of female dress codes, a form which integrates hostile and often stupidly prejudiced images of Muslims, a universalism which never seems to consider whether there might be something to be learnt *from* other cultures ... in sum, a universalism which looks like a narrow, national, blinkered French particularism.

NOTES

1. For an analysis of the work of these committees, see my 'Stasi's Republic: the school and the "veil"', December 2003-March 2004', *Modern and Contemporary France* 12:3 (2004), pp.387-97.

2. 'Les mots sont importants', or `words are important'. http://lmsi.net/

3. Sylvain Pattieu, *Les camarades des frères: trotskistes et libertaires dans la guerre d'Algérie* (Paris: Syllepsie, 2002).

4. Nestor Potkine, 'Au tour de l'Islam, maintenant', ML, 26 mai 2005.

5. Octave Mirbeau, 'To a Proletarian' in Pierre Michel and Jean-François Nivet (eds), *L'Affaire Dreyfus* (Paris: Séguier, 1991), pp.74-80.

6. Jean-Claude Richard, 'Ecole et laïcité: le débat est loin d'être tranché', ML, 21 April 2005.

7. Georges Lecardinet, 'L'appel ... ou la voix des amis de Ramadan', ML, 28 April 2005.

8. Simon, 'La laïcité n'est pas l'athéisme', ML 2 June 2005. This argument is developed at greater length by Olivier Roy, *La laïcité face à l'Islam* (Paris: Stock, 2005).

9. Cathérine Deudon, Liliane Kaudel, Annie Sugier and Anne Zelensky, 'Les féministes se dévoilent', ML, 11 Dec 2003.

10. Roland Breton, 'Le port du voile est à replacer parmi les autres pratiques sexuelles', ML, 15 Jan 2004.

11. Johann, 'La religion opprime, l'Etat réprime', ML, 22 Jan 2004.

12. 'Le Furet', 'La nouvelle bataille du voile', ML, 4 Nov 2004.

13. In this respect, the ML's coverage was markedly inferior to that provided by the libertarian-minded web-site, Les mots sont importants. See its report 'L'interdiction du voile: qu'en pensent les élèves?', dated 14 Jan 2004.

14. Tahar Ben Jelloun, *Hospitalité française: racisme et immigration maghrébine* (Paris: Seuil, 1984), p.106.

15. This new wave of Muslim thinkers is analysed by Rachid Benzine, *Les nouveaux penseurs de l'Islam* (Paris: Albin Michel, 2004). This work is not referred to in any of ML's articles.

16. D. Bouzar and S. Kada, *L'une voilée, l'autre pas* (Paris: Albin Michel, 2003).

17. Roland Breton, 'Le port du voile est à replacer parmi les autres pratiques sexuelles', ML, 15 Jan 2004.

18. On this point, see Richard Cleminson, 'Making Sense of the Body: Anarchism, Nudism and Subjective Experience', *Bulletin of Spanish Studies* 81:6 (2004), pp.697-716.

19. 'La nouvelle bataille du voile', ML, 4 Nov 2004; 'Les féministes se dévoilent', ML, 11 déc 2003.

20. 'Le Furet', 'La nouvelle bataille du voile', ML, 4 Nov 2004.

21. Roland Breton, 'Le port du voile est à replacer parmi les autres pratiques sexuelles', ML, 15 Jan 2004.

22. Nestor Potkine, 'Au tour de l'islam, maintenant', ML, 26 May 2005. One notes in passing the similarity between these ideas and those of Samuel Huntington: 'The underlying problem for the West is not Islamic fundamentalism. It is Islam, a different civilization whose people are convinced of the superiority of their culture and are obsessed with the inferiority of their power.' *The Clash of Civilizations and the Remaking of World Order* (London: Simon and Schuster, 1997), p.217.

23. On this point see Harold B. Barclay, 'Islam, Muslim Societies and Anarchy', *Anarchist Studies* 10:2 (2002), pp.105-18 and Patricia Crone, 'Ninth-Century Muslim Anarchists', *Past and Present* 167 (2000), pp.3-28. Another paradoxical similarity between anarchists and Muslims is suggested in Michael Collyer, 'Secret Agents: Anarchists, Islamists and responses to politically active refugees in London', *Ethnic and Racial Studies* 28:2 (2005), pp.278-303.

24. On cultural globalization: see Arjun Appadurai, *Modernity at Large: Cultural Dimensions of Globalization* (Minneapolis: University of Minnesota, 1996), particularly pp.21-23.

25. On asylum policy, see Carl Levy, 'The European Union after 9/11: the Demise of a Liberal Democratic Asylum Regime', *Government and Opposition* (2005), pp.26-59

26. Jean-Claude Richard, 'Le voile n'est pas soluble dans l'anarchisme', ML 27 Jan 2005.

Some thoughts on 'The Trial of Fatima'

NEIL MACMASTER

I am in overall agreement with Sharif Gemie's critique of those articles in the *Monde Libertaire* that support conservative government legislation banning the Islamic headscarf in French state schools. But there are some points that I would like to expand upon.

Sharif concludes by quoting Jean-Claude Richard to show that the ML intolerance rests upon deeply embedded traditions of *laïcité* and universalism that refuse to accept group cultural difference in the public sphere.[1] Since the headscarves controversy first kicked-off in 1989 many French intellectuals, both of the right and left, have agreed that 'communalism', the recognition of separate ethnic-group identities, subverts egalitarianism and weakens the cohesiveness of the nation-state through an internal 'balkanisation'.[2] Ethno-political organisations, it is argued, inevitably enter into conflict and competition for limited resources and lead to a situation like that of the USA, the most detested dystopia, a society divided by warring ethnic factions, ghet-toisation and 'race wars'. The ML contributors fall squarely into this 'main-stream' and seem unable to bring any self-critical awareness to the outmoded Republican model that underpins their thinking.

First, let's look a bit closer at the Richard text. Richard argues that colonialism had always deployed divide-and-rule strategies: notably, supporting 'backward' forms of culture to help reinforce domination 'by maintaining the inequalities internal to the colonial space'. Algeria, he notes, provides a key example since the colonial power reinforced the 'slavery' imposed on Muslim women, their abject submission to males, polygamy, repudiation, physical violence, seclusion and other horrors. Those who today support the right to wear the veil in French schools, derided as 'imbecile islamo-gauchistes', show a deep continuity with this 'sickening colonial history'.

This is not only poor history, but an astonishing and perverse distortion. Between c.1900 and 1962 both British and French imperialism launched a frontal attack on the perceived barbarism of 'native' Islamic culture and, centrally, repeated attempts to end veiling. This was to reach a peak during the Algerian War (1954-62), when the Psychological Warfare Bureau of the occupying army mounted a massive propaganda campaign through the radio, cinema and posters and orchestrated un-veiling ceremonies to end the practice. The aim of such policies, as Frantz Fanon and others have shown, was to attack the nationalists of the FLN by penetrating into the family cell and gaining intelligence, but the whole drive was advertised as a 'civilizing mission' for the 'emancipation' and 'modernization' of benighted Muslim women.[3] The

French colonial agenda was crucially legitimated by a discourse of universalism, that 'barbaric' Islamic practices should give way to *égalité* and *liberté*, fundamental rights shared by all humanity. Jean-Claude Richard's argument seems, then, to reveal a far deeper continuity with colonialism, Orientalism and cultural imperialism than the 'imbeciles' he derides. As Sharif notes, the universalism of the ML is a 'very peculiar form': what it assumes to be right and best for the world in reality conceals a western and French-specific model of cultural practices.

Second, the ML contributors do not seem to recognize the extent to which the debate on the Muslim veil has been driven, if not manufactured, by dubious political forces. If we look at the anti-veiling campaigns that have appeared in the western media in the last quarter of a century, it seems clear that they have never been driven by an 'objective' problem of tens of thousands of burqa-clad Muslim women pouring into public spaces. Rather they have been generated by reactionary politicians. The pattern was set a century ago by Lord Cromer, consul general of Egypt (1882-1907), who while attacking veiling and 'the degradation of women in the East', was a rabid opponent of female emancipation in England.[4] During the American invasion of Afghanistan the wife of President Bush showed a similar and unexpected progressive conscience when she made a key-note speech on the central importance of liberating Muslim women from the burqa.

Until 1989 there had been no problem in France of Muslim girls attending school in headscarves. Then the headmaster of a secondary school in Creil (who went on to build a political career as a conservative deputy) banned three girls. The furious controversy that erupted was eventually calmed by a ruling of the Council of State in November 1989 that gave a right to display religious beliefs in state schools, as long as the symbols did not constitute 'an act of pressure, proselytizing or propaganda'. Yet the conservative government was determined not to let this issue rest and brought in legislation that triggered further conflict.

At each stage in the 'battle of the veil' the media has generated massively distorted representations of Muslim girls. For example, nearly all of them wore western clothing (jeans, trainers ...) and only a modest headscarf, but instead of showing their photographs the press constantly used images from Iran and elsewhere of head-to-toe chadors, the most 'scary' and 'alien' types. The media (and here I would disagree with Sharif) also deliberately used terms like 'chador', 'burqa', 'hidjab', 'khiemar' to evoke feelings of alienation in the readership, and avoided the most accurate translation and more familiar term 'headscarf' (preferable to 'veil', which suggests a face-cover). Contributors to ML have engaged in a similar process by deliberately referring to, and confusing, the horrors of Taliban, Algerian and Iranian Islamist practices with the events in the French *banlieue*. The girls who wear Muslim symbols are on the whole freely opting to do so within a context that is radically different from, and for reasons that have little to do with, the authoritarian and patriarchal societies of North Africa or the Middle East. Richard and others widely quote the experience of Chahdorrt Djavann – an experience that derives from ten years under the veil in repressive Iran. As Sharif notes, there is barely any attempt by ML to ask young Muslim women raised in France for their point of view and why they choose to wear the veil.

In recent weeks the French government and doctrinaire proponents of *laïcité* have proclaimed the success of the Stasi law of 15 March 2004 by the argument that 'calm' now reigns in schools and the number of incidents relating to girls wearing headscarves has almost disappeared, showing a further decline on the 639 registered cases in the academic year 2004-5.[5] But this 'victory' conceals the fact that the number of Muslim girls who wore the headscarf was always below 1 percent, and the 639 incidents represent about 0.3 percent of Muslim girls of school age. What we have been witnessing is the whipping up of an enormous controversy, a deepening of public anxiety, over a tiny number of instances that offer no kind of threat to the cohesion or integrity of French society and culture.

On 29 September 2005 Asma Jahangir, a prominent human rights lawyer acting as a UN special rapporteur on freedom of religion or belief, announced findings of her investigation of the French case. The Stasi ban had led to abuses that

provoked feelings of humiliation, in particular among young Muslim women ... such public humiliation can only lead to radicalisation ... Moreover, stigmatisation of the so-called Islamic headscarf has triggered a wave of religious intolerance when women wear it outside school, at university or at their place of work.

The Stasi act has helped reinforce Islamophobia across Europe. The Dutch immigration minister, the hard-liner Rita Verdonk, has called for a ban on the 'burqa' in the interest of public safety, while the Minister of Education, Maria van der Hoeven, has called for a ban in schools – even though she admitted that she was unaware of any such veiling being worn by pupils or teachers. The Utrecht City Council has voted to cut benefits for unemployed Muslim women refusing to unveil on the grounds it prevents them finding work – an instance of punishing the victim, rather than racist employers. The Danish minister for Refugees, Immigration and Integration, Rikke Huishoj, has now spoken of following the Dutch example, as has the German state of North Rhine-Westphalia. In September 2005 Naoul Chliah was illegally prevented by officials in the town hall of Metz from attending her brother's wedding since she was wearing a headscarf. In the autumn of 2004 Giacarlo Gentilini, extreme-right wing member of the Lega Nord and mayor of Tréviso in Italy, issued a directive prohibiting women from covering their face, part of his widely publicized campaign as 'sheriff' to preserve his town from 'the foreign invasion'. Consequently, a woman of Bangladeshi origin was arrested while taking her son to school for the 'offence' of wearing a burqa, although she won a court appeal in August 2005. And so it goes on, with similar moves in Russia and elsewhere.

Following the massive demonstrations in suburban France in October and November last year, many commentators have noted that the French Republican model of integration has failed and now requires a radical rethink. While I do not accept, as has often been smugly implied, that British multiculturalism has in comparison been successful, certainly there is a need for France to examine more critically how it might implement progressive policies that can begin to end the social exclusion of ethnic minorities. It is time that contributors to *Monde Libertaire* reflected on why it is that they keep company with such strange bedfellows as Stasi and Le Pen on the issue of Muslim women. This reflection must include a rethink of discrimination in the fields of employment, housing, justice and 'ghettoisation', and of the crucial importance of the richly diverse and dynamic forms of cultural expression for minority youth to assert their identity within, not outside, French society.

NOTES

1. Jean-Claude Richard, 'Le voile n'est pas soluble dans l'anarchisme', ML 27 January 2005.

2. See Gilles Kepel, *Allah in the West* (Polity, 1997) for a typical academic attack on 'communalism'.

3. See Frantz Fanon's chapter 'Algeria unveiled' in *Studies in a Dying Colonialism* (Earthscan, 1989), 35-67.

4. Leila Ahmed, 'The discourse of the Veil' in *Women and Gender in Islam* (Yale University Press, 1992), 144-68.

5. *Le Monde*, 29 September 2005.

Comment on 'The Trial of Fatima: Anarchists, Muslims and the *Monde Libertaire*'

HAROLD B. BARCLAY

I can understand that anarchists might express extreme misgivings about the Islamic tradition which has for so long and so often been associated with authoritarian social structures. I also recognize that, given the history of the Roman Catholic Church's relationship with the French state and the struggle for secularization, present day French might be sensitive to even the slightest hint of religious behaviour within secular-operated state institutions. But let me here offer a few remarks about Islam and some observations about the French and their relations with their North African population.

We should not forget, as Sharif Gemie points out, that Islam is not a monolithic system and that it incorporates a variety of views. And even in its toleration and accommodation to authoritarian politics, the religious system is highly decentralized, lacking any central authority. Thus, while one jurist may prepare a *fatwa* or opinion condemning contraception, another may prepare one which permits it. Although the Iranian Shiites may be somewhat more rigidly structured, they still have several *ayatollas* and numerous *mujtahids* who have the right to interpret Islamic teaching directly from the Qur'an (in contrast to Sunnis who may only do so directly from the Shari'a). The *ayatollas* are traditionally seen as equals and above ordinary *mujtahids*.

As Gemie also suggests, Muslim tradition has made many important contributions to humanity. However, its contribution has more often than not been in the role of a transmitter of ideas rather than the producer of highly original ones. Thus, both algebra and the zero – to cite two widely know examples – were adopted from Indian tradition and passed on to the West, although Muslims were responsible for a considerable elaboration of algebra from its much less developed source. Similarly our knowledge of ancient Greek thought would be poor indeed if it were not for the fact that Muslims preserved their achievements and transmitted them to the West.

To add to Sharif's observations, one might note that there is a clear social gospel which proposes an economy which is neither precisely capitalist or non-capitalist but designed for an earlier time. It is a system which recognizes the right to private property and accepts differences in wealth, but which aims to set limits to exploitation and the accumulation of wealth. Of course, Islam's economic prescriptions have never been effective in providing for a just society. Yet in their attempt to apply the prohibition on charging interest Muslims have devised some interesting and sometimes rather unusual means of engaging in economic exchange. Their inheritance rules divide any legacy among a number of relatives, so as, ideally, to prevent extensive accumulation of unearned increment. Contrary to what some believe, women inherit and accumulate wealth and do not surrender their control of it to men on marriage. Rules opposing gambling include the prohibition of dealing in futures. Rules for the market place provide for fair weights and measures and protection against adulterated foods and materials. *Zakat*, the obligation to give in support of the community, seeks to provide for essentially free educational and medical institutions, and a levelling of wealth.

Having said all of this, I do not wish to be seen as an apologist for Islam but to indicate, along with Sharif, that all things Muslim are not evil, as our latter day Manichaeans would have it.

Now, I wish to proceed to the question of the relation between the French population and its Muslim minority. The general French attitude towards its Muslim population in regard to appropriate dress and the overall role of North Africans within French society reflects a thoroughly negative if not racist view. That some French anarchists express support for the legal prohibition of headscarves is, it seems to me, clearly contrary to anarchist theory and practice for it means that they favour the enforcement by the state of the regulation of dress, which is not a notion at all compatible with anarchism. As Sharif has observed, little or no consideration has been given to the Muslim women's perceptions of the veil. The only thing that seems to count is an arbitrary Western notion that it is a form of oppression, irrespective of the fact that those who wear the scarf may not think so at all.

Appropriate dress is a problem which has arisen in other communities. As is well known, a Sikh male is expected to allow his hair to grow, to wear a turban and to carry a ceremonial knife. The tradition aroused some concern in the non-Sikh community in parts of Canada and the United States and it remains problematical in jurisdictions where laws have been passed requiring the wearing of protective helmets while riding a bicycle and, in others, prohibiting knives in schools. But Sikhs are permitted to wear turbans (though some Canadian legion branches have demanded that turbans be removed on entering their halls); and in early 2005 New York City passed legislation protecting the right of Sikhs to wear turbans and Muslim women to wear headscarves. At the same time, it is apparently uncontroversial for Amish and conservative Mennonite women to wear prayer caps: there are several areas in the United States and Canada where members of these sects are a very visible minority. Above all, one could look to India where all manner of dress is tolerated, including nudity, for the most 'holy' members of the Digambara ('the Sky-clad') sect of Jains never wear any clothes. It is disturbing to think that so many people on this earth can be so much more tolerant of modes of dress than some anarchists and the French public. When it was pointed out to officials in the French Ministry of Education that there were 15,000 Sikhs in France the response was: 'What? There are Sikhs in France'? – further suggesting that the issue could have been more fully explored.

In France it has been observed that a prohibition on the wearing of cruci-fixes by Catholics and yarmulkas by Jews in public schools will have little effect on the children involved because only the most conservative Catholics wear prominent crucifixes and the most orthodox Jews wear yarmulkas. Most if not all of these would be attendants at private religious schools. It is argued that the law about 'religious' dress is, therefore, primarily directed to discrim-inating against Muslims, since they are most likely to attend the public school where the law would apply. Further, as the Voice of Asia-Pacific Network has said, the crucifix is worn as 'a matter of religious expression' while the headscarf, like the Sikh turban and the yarmulka, is often worn as part of 'strict religious adherence'.

Events in Paris and its suburbs in November 2005 reveal major crises that are likely to be more important than the dispute over headscarves. On the encouragement of the French government and French corporations, most of the North African residents of the Paris slums came to France to take jobs not filled by the French. As Doug Ireland argues, the available jobs were more in the realm of menial tasks and most of the immigrants were put into cheap, high rise housing ghettos ...

> specially built for them, and deliberately placed out of sight in the suburbs around most of France's major urban agglomerations, so that the darker-skinned inhabitants wouldn't pollute the center cities of Paris, Lyon, Toulouse, Lille, Nice and the others of white France's urban centers today encircled by flames. Often there was only just enough public transport provided to ... take them to work but few linking the ghettos to urban centers.
>
> Now 30, 40 and 50 years old, these high-rise human warehouses in the isolated suburbs are today run-down, dilapidated, sinister places, with broken elevators that remain unrepaired, heating systems left dysfunc-tional in winter, dirt and dog-shit in the hallways, broken windows, and few commercial amenities – shopping for basic necessities is often quite limited and difficult, while entertainment and recreational facilities for youth are truncated and totally inadequate when they're not non-existent (D. Ireland, 2005).

Nicholas Sarkozy, Minister of Religion, denounces the ghetto rebel youth in the most abusive manner, calls for repression, and declares the violence is 'centrally organized'. However, others have said there is no central organiza-tion – '... the rebellion is spreading because the youth have a sense of solidarity' – and a system of networking. It is spreading 'spontaneously – driven especially by racist police conduct ...' (D Ireland, 2005). It would be interesting to know to what extent the French anarchists who support the government's repression of Muslim headscarves also approve of the general treatment accorded the North African population. Given this present rebellion, whose ultimate causes rest with the French government and French corporations, it may transpire that the headscarf issue will recede into the background, although it seems clear that all these matters are related, at least by one thing – widespread French antipathy towards Africans and Muslims.

ENDNOTE

1. Isn't it rather contradictory that the French secular state should have a Minister of Religion?

BIBLIOGRAPHY

Ireland, Doug, 'Why is France Burning?: The Rebellion of a Lost Generation', blog DIRELAND, reported in 'Truthout', November 6, 2005.

Some observations on Sharif Gemie's essay

GEORGES UBBIALI

Member of Editorial Committee of *Dissidences* – writing in a personal capacity

I was extremely interested in Sharif Gemie's essay, and I find that I am largely in agreement with his ideas. Before presenting some criticisms and some support, however, one point must be made concerning the material from which his analysis is drawn. This type of debate requires a far broader investigation: after all, the 'veil affair' began in 1989.

Let us begin with my main criticism, which concerns the passages at the end of the article, debating the issue of manipulation and the role of Islamist organizations, above all of the UOIF. I do not share his view that this organization can be seen as a legitimate player in this contest. Even if this organization, and others like it, act within the framework of the law, it still remains the case that there cannot be any form of solidarity with them. Any progressive form of politics must fight the UOIF and all other fundamentalist organizations. Just as it is unacceptable to propose any solidarity whatsoever with anti-semites who defend the Palestinian cause, so there can be no compromise with the reactionary principles represented by the UOIF and their associates. It is clear that they have tried to exploit the issue of the veil. They must be denounced, and it has to be stated that these are organizations to be opposed. There cannot be any sympathy for any reactionary forces, whether they are Arab or Islamic. But let us be clear: this is not a question of denouncing Islam, but of refusing those currents who base themselves on this religion and who draw from it a political culture which is incompatible with progressive ideals.

Aside from this point, Gemie's essay has the great virtue of giving the 'Union Sacrée' that the ML has joined a good kicking.[1] (It's worth remembering that this is not the first time that libertarians have allowed themselves to be carried along by a 'Union Sacrée'). In fact, an astonishing national coalition has been formed to denounce the threat to *laïcité* represented by the veil, which stretches from the far right to the far left (including the libertarians of the FA, but not those of Alternative Libertaire; the Trotskyists of Parti des travailleurs and Lutte ouvrière, but not those of the Ligue Communiste révolutionnaire). Such unanimity in denouncing young women of Arab origin as threat to the foundations of the Republic has never been seen before. Nobody seems to ask why, for over a decade, not a single pupil wearing a Christian symbol, a Jewish kippa or a symbol of any other religion, has ever, *ever*, been expelled from a French state school. (Let us note in passing that none of the defenders of the threatened Republic seems to worry about, or to protest about, the fact that the young veiled women are usually accepted, with their veils, in private or religious schools.) The presence of a few young veiled women in school has created an outcry among the standard-bearers of *laïcité*. But have they ever protested about the special status of the eastern region of Alsace-Lorraine, which makes Catholic, religious education compulsory for all children? Have they ever protested about the chaplains which can be found in many state schools across France? Let us remember that the Stasi Commission said nothing about these topics.

Legal exclusion from school cannot be a proper response to the veil. However, I have no wish to suggest that I accept the wearing of the veil. If it is likely that there are several different meanings to veil,[2] it remains true that one cannot accept this symbol of female submission. The veil is a negation of a woman as an autonomous individual. However, repressing those who are the victims of the veil will never lead to the end of this subordination. Instead, we must trust the state school, its teachers, the dynamic of liberation-by-knowledge which it transmits, and the emancipating power of education to oppose religious obscurantism. School exclusions are fair responses to some forms of behaviour which are unacceptable: for example, the refusal to attend classes such as gymnastics (where some have said that they will refuse to show their bodies) or biology (because of the references to human reproduction) or any other classes which present forms of knowledge which clash with religious precepts. But in this debate we are not debating values so much as universal considerations (or considerations which are as universal as possible): the acquisition of cognitive knowledge. ML has not noticed that within this debate there is a latent issue: 'should we accept immigrants from north Africa in France?'.[3] Instead, it has thrown itself into the stampede, grasping onto reactionary interpretations of *laïcité*.

NOTES

1. The 'Union Sacrée' was the wartime coalition of left-wing, centrist and right-of-centre parties formed in 1914.
2. See, for example, F. Gaspard and F. Khosrokhavar, *Le foulard et la république*, (Découverte, 1995).
3. Pierre Bourdieu, 'Un problème peut en cacher un autre' in Nordmann Charlotte (ed) *Le foulard islamique en questions* (Amsterdam, 2004) pp.45-46.

The shadows of the enlightenment: some Foucaultian perspectives on the French law and the veil

BELTRÁN ROCA

Department of Social and Cultural Anthropology
University of Seville
Member of the CNT

Globalization and the social transformations which stem from what Anthony Giddens has termed 'late modernity' highlight the limits of the social structures and systems of thought that were devised in the early stages of modernity. Both the ideologies (by which I mean more-or-less coherent bodies of ideas/beliefs) and the organizations which embody them are products of a particular social-cultural context. As history develops they change, adapt, rise to power, enter into crisis and then die. Like liberalism or Marxism, anarchism is a system of thought which has its roots in the Enlightenment. This means that many of its ideas are now either out-dated or unable to meet the challenges of today's society. The debate concerning ML's response to the French government's decision to ban the wearing of the veil in state schools gives us a welcome opportunity to reconsider many of the preconceptions and accepted ideas which form the theoretical apparatus of an important section of the anarchist movement. Some of these ideas are responsible for the theoretical dead end in which the libertarian movement finds itself.

As Sharif Gemie explains, during 2003 and 2004 a vigorous polemic developed within the French state concerning the prohibition in state schools of clothes or symbols which were *ostensiblement* religious, such as the Islamic veil, the Jewish *kippa* and Christian crosses 'of excessive size'. The government's main argument was that state schooling must be secular and, therefore, that religious symbols have no place in it. Under the cover of *laïcité*, the government knew full well what it implied: it would reinforce the integration of ethnic minorities by assimilation – that is to say, through the imposition of the host country's culture. There are two inter-related dimensions to this debate: (i) *laïcité* – the opposition to religiosity and (ii) the response of western culture to cultural diversity. I will argue that the French libertarian movement has failed to respond properly to this issue and that it has wrongly placed itself alongside the supporters of the law.

The misunderstanding of issues – *laïcité* and cultural contestation – is rooted in an uncritical acceptance of attitudes inherited directly from the French Revolution. The term 'late modernity' attempts to capture our position in a historical moment and describes some of the ways in which key aspects of modernity have undergone significant transformations. Many of modernity's principles are now questioned: faith in human progress, rationality and productivism are no longer regarded as necessary 'goods'. For example it is now acknowledged that scientific advances have not always produced improvements in people's lives and that they have sometimes served as instruments of oppression.

Secularization is another pillar of modernity (Moreno, 2002) and can be understood as a process in which religion loses its central place in society. The fathers of sociology mapped advances in scientific knowledge against the disappearance of magical and religious thinking. Max Weber spoke of the 'disenchantment' of the world; Comte anticipated the positivist stage in human development where society would re-organize itself through science. Today, we can see that these processes are uncertain. On the one hand, traditional religions still have as many followers – if not more – as they did centuries ago. On the other, religious culture has become fragmented: there are a variety of groups competing in the 'market' for the salvation of souls (Bourdieu, 2000). As Manuela Cantón (2001: 234) notes, 'rather than seeing the increasingly strong dynamic of contemporary religious creativity as a sign of an irrational revival ... let us understand the fragmentation of the religious words as a sign of an important metamorphosis', in which the models we have inherited from the Enlightenment must be revised or replaced.

The Enlightenment placed the individual at the centre of its concept of 'rights'. In practice, all Western legislation was aimed at individuals. Yet there is a growing demand that states recognize collective or cultural rights, as the native Indian movement in Latin America and other ethnic nationalisms show (Stavenhagen, 2005: 29). Through these rights, the lifestyles of ethnic minorities, the aspiration to self-government for particular ethnic groups, traditional forms of conflict resolution, and the traditional territories and authorities of indigenous communities would all enjoy a degree of legal protection.

To date, this demand has met a cautious institutional response, though the UN's *Human Development Report* for 2004 stressed the need to preserve cultural diversity and to adopt political strategies which encourage cultural liberty, linguistic pluralism, traditional knowledge, etc. Moreover, in reality globalization – understood as the imposition on a planetary scale of a single model of society dominated by the logic of the market – constitutes a serious threat to these rights, as it has a levelling effect, converting all into a commodity whose value will be determined by the law of supply and demand. As Rudolf Rocker observed, uniformity and expansion are the foundations of all forms of power.

> The dream of creating a universal empire is not a phenomenon of ancient history; it is the logical result of all forms of power ... The aspiration to unify everything, to submit all social movements to a central will, is the basis of all power (Rocker, 1977: 70-71).

From the words of this celebrated anarchist, we can conclude that the libertarian opposition to power can be understood as the defence of cultural or religious identity as a guarantee of a valuable diversity. If we re-consider the Enlightenment roots of libertarian thinking and revise these ideas in the light of the problems they now pose, we will be able to devise tactics that will enable us successfully to meet today's dilemmas.

Once the right to cultural diversity has been recognized, how will different groups relate to each other? The position taken by European governments in favour of *laïcité* is the separation of the government of peoples in the public sphere from the government of souls in the private. This separation might seem a reasonable proposal: and yet inter-group relations are difficult, and require negotiation. The cultural relativism that anthropology teaches is a necessary instrument for creating a model of co-existence: all social practices, even the most repulsive, are equally human and can be understood in cultural terms. Yet it is not sufficient. Such relativism, if taken to extremes, can generate a dangerous, reactionary result: it can produce a complete absence of values. This is where we, as citizens, can and must defend some of the values shaped by the Enlightenment: liberty, equality and fraternity. The question that confronts us with the issue of the veil is that it is not clear whether it constitutes a threat to those values or if it is actually an affirmation of the same values.

CONCEALMENT AND DOMINATION: THE BODY AS AN OBJECT OF POLITICS

In his *Discipline and Punish*, Michel Foucault (2000) shows us that there was a fundamental change in the manner in which power was exercised at the end of the eighteenth century and the start of the nineteenth. In western societies, sovereign power, exercised mainly through the spectacular rituals of torture, was replaced by disciplinary power. This consisted of modelling and manipulating bodies and minds by diverse techniques such as supervision and examination. Today, such disciplines are still central elements of our societies: such power constructs the individual, and the body is an object of politics.

The anarchists' big mistake is to consider that power can only be exercised in a negative form. Instead, power can also reveal and produce.[1] Foucault begins the first volume of his *History of Sexuality* by noting that the popular argument that sexuality is something prohibited or taboo is completely false. Instead, Foucault argues, sexuality is a topic of endless debate. The discursive multiplication of sexuality is apparent in just a few moments of television: adverts for cars, holidays or deodorants are based on the promise of sexual success; near-naked women – and, increasingly, men – are ever-present; reality shows in which contestants seduce and are seduced have become a common feature of the schedules. More examples could be given. The machinery that produces this hyper-reality sweats sexuality from every pore.

Sharif Gemie has noted in his essay that it is false to consider that displaying one's body is synonymous with liberation and that hiding one's body means repression. He is not wrong. Moving to the specific issue of the veil, there is a similar problem in arguing that its use must signify repression. Following Foucault, it must be remembered that power can be exercised in both hidden and open forms. Everything depends on the meaning of such acts. For the Spanish anarchists of the early twentieth century, nudism was a means by which to liberate oneself from the corset of Catholic morality. It was also a way of reconciling oneself with nature, and of producing a utopian experience. On the other hand, for prostitutes in the red light district of Amsterdam or for strippers, for example, nudity could well be experienced as a type of repression.[2] Something similar is happening with the young women who put on veils: for them, it is a clear symbol of an identity in the strongest and most positive sense of the word. The veil represents what they are: Muslim women. To deny them the right to wear it is to deny them the right to be themselves. For this reason, one of them shaved her head as a sign of protest, as if to say 'without the veil I am nothing'.[3]

Power does not simply prohibit: it also creates pleasure, pain, knowledge, structures, organizations, discourses and individuals. Power is necessary, and the challenge facing anarchists is not to eliminate it, but to direct it in such a way that it is not autonomous from society – as the prehistoric hunter-gatherers did (Morris, 2005 and Graeber, 2004).

THE AMBIVALENCE OF RELIGION

Veiling is not so much a religious ritual as a cultural practice. Yet as soon as religion enters the debate, it ceases to be a side issue.

Once again, Foucault (1984) offers us some approaches to this issue. According to his 'law of the tactical polyvalence of discourses', each discourse can be understood as a multiplicity of elements that can contribute to different strategies. Different discursive elements enter into play within power structures. Different – and even contradictory – discourses can contribute to a single strategy; rival strategies can use similar discourses. There are no simple binaries and it is simplistic to argue that there is one libertarian discourse and another repressive one, which legitimates oppression: to argue in this sense merely reproduces the juridical image of power.

Aside from the practical consequences of a belief in the existence of God, religion is just another signifying system along with so many others.[4] Durkheim (2003) demonstrated in his work on totemism in Australia that religion is concerned with issues in the 'here and now': it fulfils functions of social cohesion and the explanation of reality.

Religion – Christianity, Islam or any other – constitutes a polyvalent discourse: it is not the 'opium of the people' that Marx identified, nor is it an instrument of redemption as its defenders claim. An anthropological approach to religion, which studies it in its socio-cultural and political contexts, shows that religious discourses have served the oppressed classes' desire for subversion as much as the ruling classes' need for legitimacy.[5] Anarchist militants have often forgotten this point. Rocker, however, saw Christianity as originally a 'revolutionary movement of the masses, whose doctrine of the equality of all beings in the sight of God subverted the basis of the Roman state' (Rocker, 1977: 72). He adds that Christianity was persecuted precisely in order to eradicate its anti-statist arguments. But when Constantine declared Christianity as the official state religion, its original aspiration slowly disappeared, despite the continuing opposition of groups such as the Manicheans and Chiliasts.

Like Christianity, Islam contains a multiplicity of liberatory elements: it is all a question of the interpretations and significations which social actors grant it in each specific context.

WOMEN'S RIGHTS AND ETHNOCENTRISM

The arguments presented above suggest that covering one's head does not signify submission, but is an assertion of identity. One should therefore question the causes of the recent offensive against Muslim women. I would suggest that the media's flood of images concerning the difficulties facing Muslim women is due to western ethno-centrism. This arrogant belief in western superiority is also professed by many anarchist militants, as the articles in ML demonstrate.

If one talks of *the* difficult situation of *the* Muslim woman, completely subordinate to men, one simplistically ignores the real heterogeneity of situations in which these women live, the differences caused by governments, ethnic identities, social class and age. One also hides the dreadful lives of many western women, whether victims of their husband's violence, exhibited as objects, or taking poorly paid jobs.

In order to understand this richly exploited flood of images concerning oppressed Muslim women, it is useful to place it in its political, economic and social context. In reality, the EU has been constructed as a fortress. It aims to be unassailable, and it protects its privileged citizens from those who come from other lands – particularly from Africa. This vast process of exclusion demands cultural, ideological, philosophical and historical legitimation. Authors like Sartori (2001) or Huntington (1996) speak of a supposed 'clash of civilizations' which threatens world peace, and for which the only solution is the imposition of western hegemony over Islam and China. Historians are beginning to develop a so-called 'history of Europe', presenting the region as an historical reality, and forgetting that it is a construct of very recent times. It is in this context that the western discourses on Islam are being produced: and the situation of women provides the perfect illustration of the apparent differences between the two cultures.

Many forget that it is precisely these Muslim women, many of them wearing the veil, who are the real agents of change in their societies. They forget that Islam, a polyvalent discourse, open to interpretation, can also be used strategically to defend women's rights and fight patriarchy. Happily, a growing Islamic feminism reminds us that one can be a Muslim and fight patriarchy, or any other form of domination.

CONCLUSION

The response of the French anarchist movement to the veil, as revealed in ML, is completely mistaken. For French Muslim women the veil is not a religious sign, but a cultural one. The French government has used the rhetoric of *laïcité* to launch an attack on the cultural rights of ethnic minorities. This issue suggests that we must question and revise some of the ideas that the libertarian tradition has inherited from the Enlightenment, and that we must adopt a more creative analysis of contemporary social processes, based on further consideration of questions such as the polyvalence of religion, the oppressive potential of science, the limits to rationality, the importance of ethnic identity, cultural relativism (and its risks), the significance of the body in the exercise of power, the weaknesses of the anarchist concept of power and the different interpretations of *laïcité*. This renovation of anarchist discourse is essential if it is to respond to the new challenges of globalization.

NOTES

1. Pierre Bourdieu's celebrated formula that television hides by exhibiting aptly captures the idea (1996: 24).

2. I will not attempt to engage in the controversial debate between proponents of the legalization of prostitution, and supporters of its abolition. This debate is extremely complex and often fruitless, merely serving to divide, once more, resistance to patriarchal power.

3. Let us note in passing that shaving the heads of Republican and anarchist women was a common practice in Spain after the Civil War. Cutting their hair was a way of annihilating them as people by destroying one of the key aspects of their identity: their gender. The analogy with the prohibition of the veil, as a sign of religion, ethnicity and gender, is obvious.

4. Despite the ideas which have been popularized by the libertarian movement (Faure, 1980; Lopez y Ferreras, 1996), I personally doubt whether the acceptance or not of a supreme being transforms the existence of an oppressed person.

5. An interesting study on the link between political ideology and religious beliefs in Guatemala is Pilar Sanchiz (1998), *Evangelismo y poder*.

Anarchism, anti-clericalism and religions

PAUL CHAMBERS

Centre for Border Studies
Dept. of Sociology, Forest Hall
University of Glamorgan
Pontypridd CF37 1DL

ABSTRACT

This paper explores the relationship between anarchism and religions from the perspective of the sociology of religion. I take anarchism to mean resistance to the idea and practice of state power and an affirmation of the principle of non-coercive power as the preferred foundation of social order. I view all religions as human social constructions, although as a sociologist, I also maintain a methodological agnosticism towards the various 'truth' claims of religions. I begin this discussion by outlining, from the perspective of anarchist theory, the historical relationship between anarchism and religions before a more detailed exploration, drawing from English and Welsh examples, of the linkages between religion and radical dissent. The discussion then moves to an analysis of Islam and the nature of power and authority as it is understood by Muslims before exploring recent controversies surrounding the banning of the veil in French schools, the nature of Islamaphobia, and their implications for anarchist theory and practice.

INTRODUCTION

It is currently estimated that there are 11 million Muslims living in Europe and that Muslims make up approximately three per cent of most western populations.[1] Former colonial connections account for much of this diaspora and it is increasingly clear that the Islamic presence in Europe is here to stay.[2] Moreover, this intrusion of the *other* into Western societies and cultures challenges many assumptions about European life, both past and present.[3] Sharif Gemie's timely article is also concerned with challenging assumptions. In this case, the many assumptions informing current debates in the *Monde Libertaire* about the nature and limits of *laïcité* in European societies. He suggests that this discourse is innately French in its provenance (reflecting the Gallic – and perhaps, anarchist – tradition of anti-clericalism) but that it also draws from ill-informed and stereotypical images of Muslims and Islam and a particularistic view of culture that paradoxically seeks to deny the principle of religious neutrality (and thus religious liberty) that is captured in the notion of *laïcité*. In his analysis he notes that ML's articles are mainly concerned with

Islam in relation to French schools; notably the right or the denial of that right to wear the veil for religious and cultural reasons and the law of 2004. He also suggests that the majority of these articles support the law (and by extension the state), a puzzling stance for an ostensibly anarchist publication. Moreover, from the perspective of anarchism and anarchists there is a curious suggestion that liberty might be upheld by the denial of liberty.

This paper seeks to relate Gemie's discussion to wider currents of anarchist thought, notably the need to rethink anarchism within the context of the twenty-first century and also to argue these issues from the perspective of the sociology of religion, which is my particular discipline.[4] From the latter perspective, it is clear that anarchism has a long tradition of anti-clericalism and I would argue that this tradition is partially reflected in the ambivalence demonstrated towards Islam and Muslims in many of the *Monde Libertaire* articles cited by Gemie. In terms of rethinking anarchism, I would argue that anarchists need to reconsider some of their traditional assumptions about religion and power, not least because of the contemporary global political situation where religion is increasingly (but not exclusively so) a site of protest and resistance to fascistic, militaristic and universalizing forces.[5] It is becoming increasingly clear that religion has both become more transnational in character while continuing to be a vehicle for political expression and social change in ways that are surprising to those who once expected a progressive secularization ultimately to reach every part of the globe.[6]

ANARCHIST THEORY AND ANTI-CLERICALISM

Opposition to religion has been a cornerstone of much classical anarchist theory and in revolutionary situations this hostility has often been manifested in violent forms of anti-clericalism.[7] However, this opposition needs to be contextualized. For thinkers such as Mikhail Bakunin, organized religion was a problem but only to the extent that religious power was wrapped up in state power. In as much as religion legitimized the state and its actions, it was to be resisted and if need be, destroyed.[8] In the final instance, and despite his confla-tion of church and state, Bakunin was essentially anti-state.[9] For Errico Malatesta, religion was a collective hallucination and a powerful ideology, whereby existing systems of economic relations are justified and authorities legitimated through religious institutions. Religion, therefore, is a lie and reli-gious institutions have 'no *raison d'être* except in so far as they are the result of political and economic privileges, and a means to defend and consolidate them'.[10] Both perspectives see religion and its institutions as legitimising existing authorities and powers, political and economic. Conversely, Rudolph Rocker (perhaps reflecting his association with Jewish workers) does not auto-matically write off religion and religious systems of thought.[11] As Rocker notes, there is a long historical tradition of anarchist and proto-communist thought stretching from the writings of William Godwin through to the works of Richard Hooker, Gerrard Winstanly, Algernon Sidney, John Locke, Richard Price, Robert Owen and Thomas Paine (and we might add to this list William Blake and Leo Tolstoy) that explicitly and implicitly draws inspiration from religion, albeit in unconventional and critical forms.[12]

As Gemie notes, there is a lack of sensitivity on the part of ML's contributors to 'the cultural and social role of religions' and he cites Marx's more nuanced approach. While Marx was ambivalent about religion, laying great stress on its ideological function, he simultaneously recognised its ability to offset the worse effects of alienation, particularly for social minorities. For Marx, religion is both the product of specific sets of social and economic conditions and, importantly, the ideological product of alienation.[13] The Marxist writer Otto Maduro further suggests that religion should be seen as more than a variable determined by the external and mechanical forces in play within economic systems. Concepts of base and superstructure are abstractions by which we can discern diverse social functions and not concrete classifications. Religious systems are relatively autonomous and any starting point for analysis must be located in the system itself. Only when this is understood can it be situated within the wider social structure.[14]

RELIGION AND RADICAL DISSENT

The upshot of this argument is that there is a need to distinguish between religions of power and religions of revolt. Religion can challenge as well as support the *status quo* and in Britain there is a long tradition of radical dissent linking religion to communism and other forms of socialism.[15] From the Peasants Revolt of 1381 through to The English Revolution (1640), the linkages between religious 'heresies' and political and social dissent are clear.[16] In Britain the situationist anarchist tradition identifies itself strongly with the religiously inspired popular protests known as the Gordon Riots.[17] Clearly, context is everything.

This is well illustrated by Welsh history. Wales has always been to some extent a marginalized region, politically, economically and culturally, and religion has historically been a central actor in collective resistance to English colonial domination. The Welsh reputation for collective piety did not emerge until after the Protestant Reformation and the capture of religion by the state and the subsequent establishment of a state church. Soon after, in those upland areas where state control was at its weakest, dissenting congregations independent of the established church emerged. Meeting in conditions of secrecy, they forged a new type of indigenous religion whose central organizing principle came from the people themselves.[18] Lambert has characterized these groups as 'self governing ecclesiastical republics' and this captures well the institution of 'the chapel', organized by the people for the people.[19] (The parallels with anarchist forms of organization are suggestive. These same principles also govern contemporary mosque organization in Europe).

This new social movement grew rapidly among the common people and was heavily implicated in the rural social protests that were collectively termed 'the Rebecca Riots'.[20] Further impetus came from the establishment of the South Wales coalfields and the mass movement of peoples into these newly industrialized areas. Here the chapel was a central institution in working-class life and in boom-towns such as Merthyr, religious radicalism was increasingly accompanied by political radicalism: the political force of the chapels found its fullest expression in syndicalism.[21] Syndicalism emerged as a significant force in the South Wales coalfields in the first two decades of the twentieth century.[22] This trend was deeply influenced by the establishment of close links between Welsh and American miners and many of the latter were associated with the International Workers of the World (the Wobblies). At least one Welsh political agitator operating in the coalfields during this period noted that syndicalist ideas found 'a ready made audience in the chapels'.[23] The writings of Daniel de Leon were widely disseminated and prominent agitators such as Big Bill Haywood also visited the coal fields.[24] Increasingly, home-grown figures such as Noah Ablett and Tom Evans (both members of the Plebs League) emerged from the chapels and these activists in turn helped shape (for a time) the South Wales Miners Federation (the Fed) as a radical syndicalist movement.[25] (Although he later rejected the religion of his youth, Ablett had been a noted boy preacher in the chapels of the Rhondda Valley.)[26] This socialist turn dominated the chapels well into the twentieth century and was exemplified by strong religious support for the anti-Franco movement in Spain.[27]

The point that I want to make here is that even in a society such as Wales which for a time was dominated by religion and religious ideas, it was possible for anarchist and socialist ideas to take hold and flourish, not by overt rejection of religion but by finding ways to work within that intensely religious culture. One of the most striking aspects of early syndicalist agitation in Wales was its readiness to harness specifically religious imagery to propagate a radical and progressive message.[28] The possibilities for an anarchist engagement with Muslims in Europe (and even elsewhere in the world) are real.

ISLAM

Clearly, history demonstrates that religion can be a progressive force in some economic, political and cultural contexts and that we need to distinguish between the various types and forms of religion and their relationship with political structures and the State.[29] Moreover, as I have argued above, history tells us that religion can accord with anarchist principles both ideologically and organizationally. Islam is no exception here. As Gemie notes, Harold Barclay has made some interesting observations about the possible relationships between anarchist principles and *some* Muslim societies.[30] Perhaps Barclay's most pertinent comments relate to the relationship between anarchism and authority and the ways in which authority might in some cases be justified. He suggests that 'rational' types of authority based on the principle of competence, notably the relationship between teacher and student, can be a source for empowerment and not domination and ultimately 'temporary' in nature. This accords well with Muslim notions in which authority is based upon competence, is always charismatic (in the Weberian sense) and (by virtue of the nature of charismatic authority) is essentially temporary.[31] The type of hierarchical power structures that inform the Christian religion are absent in Islam. (Rather, Islam organises itself by schools of thought.)[32] In principle, Islam eschews dogma in favour of discourse and ideological domination in favour of consensus, again something suggestive of anarchist principles. Power, if it lies anywhere, lies in the power to convince by power of argument and the ability to relate this to previous discourses in both the Qur'an and the *Hadith* literature (eyewitness traditions relating to the actions and sayings of the Prophet Muhammad).[33] Again, when we look at the way in which Muslims organize themselves religiously, there is a total absence of the type of power structures typified by western (Christian) forms of religion. There are no hierarchies of bishops, no churches, no denominations, no power structures outside the local, no domination of the local mosque by any other authorities. Muslims organize themselves locally as they wish. They fund their own mosques. They appoint their own teachers. In other words, their forms of organization would be recognizable to anyone involved in anarchist organizations.

THE VEIL

In terms of the position of women in Islam, as Barclay notes, patriarchy remains a problem. However, I would argue that this is less a problem for Islam than for the various patriarchal cultures within which Islam operates. Historically, the spread of Islam has sought to accommodate (rightly or wrongly) local cultural elements where they do not appear to overtly conflict with Islamic ideology.[34] Other sociologists suggest that differing attitudes towards women are at least partially dependent upon the different schools of *fikh*.[35] Taken together, these factors are reflected in the varying experiences of women in different Muslim societies. Simply, some Muslim groups and societies are more repressive than others. Some seek to exclude women from public life. Others seek to build separate but parallel (or pillarised) gendered spheres or structures that, in theory, offer equality of opportunity. As Gemie argues, the crucial point here is to avoid conflating the many varieties of Muslim experience into an essentially artificial and monolithic construct: Islam. Islam is not a static tradition and there are many differences of opinion and many different contexts in which issues relating to women are debated. In terms of the veil, Islamic authorities are generally agreed that there is no principle of compulsion.[36] Moreover, as Gemie notes, we should consider the experiences of real people rather than ideological systems – not least because of the well documented patterns of social exclusion that inform the daily experience of many Muslims living in Europe.

Most sociologists of religion would agree that ethnic and religious identity, and its embodiment in something like wearing the veil, is a complex phenomenon encompassing many meanings. The cultural practice of wearing the veil is a relatively modern phenomenon, with no specific historical precedents, although in general, it conforms to Qur'anic principles of modesty in dress. (It is worth noting that Muslim men are also 'subject' to proscriptions in appearance.) In practice, there are any number of variations in approaches to veiling, reflecting diverse theological understandings of *fikh* and the inherited cultural and social traditions that migrant ethnic groups bring from their territorial points of origin, as well as positioning in terms of class and economics and in relation to the norms and values of the host society. As with all cultural practices that draw from traditional sources, there is inevitably some tension between the principles of voluntarism and compulsion, and any analysis should be sensitive to this and to the meanings that individuals and groups (and others) apply to their social actions. This lack of agreement (both within and without the European Islamic community) as to the cultural significance of the veil has led to a lively debate. The veil has been viewed variously as an expression of personal spirituality, a symbolic marker of cultural identity, a duty incumbent on Muslim women, a signifier of intolerance, an expression of patriarchal control and as a cultural symbol denoting a refusal to integrate into western societies.[37]

It is clear that any realistic analysis of the veiling of women must recognise that the options for choice in this matter may well be limited for many Muslim women living in Europe. On the other hand, it is also abundantly clear that an increasing number of young women (particularly those of the second and third generations of migrant families) are voluntarily choosing to adopt the veil. In some cases, where families have consciously chosen the path of assimilation into the secular host society, the decision to adopt the veil can come as a shock, attracting parental disapproval. Clearly, in these cases (and there are many) familial coercion is not a factor. Moreover, there is much sociological research that would suggest that even where families are supportive of traditional practices, their children are often acutely aware of the difference between cultural traditions as understood by their parents (arranged marriages, the seclusion of women, the wearing of the *bhurka*) and the very minimal requirements laid down in the Qur'an.[38]

Again, the decision to adopt the veil in western societies cannot be seen outside the very real raft of social pressures to conform to a society that simultaneously marginalizes Muslims and their culture, and the exclusionary practices in education and employment that follow on from this. In these cases, and as many young Muslim women argue, the decision to adopt the veil can be a personally liberating experience; a rejection of the claims of the dominant metropolitan culture, a rejection of the male gaze and the objectification of the female body and an affirmation of the principle of liberty in religious matters. The crucial point here is that we should pay attention to the subjective dispositions of social actors. Clearly, not all Muslim women adopt the veil through coercion. For many it is a matter of free choice. It is not enough to say that the choices Muslim women make in their lives, whether to wear the veil or not, are simply the product of false consciousness. For anarchists to argue this is to fall into the trap of Leninism, what Gemie describes as 'an assumption of intellectual and political superiority'. Anarchist thought is not necessarily privileged over other systems of thought and anarchists do not constitute a vanguard leadership.

ISLAMAPHOBIA

When we consider the 2004 law we also need to consider contexts. It is perfectly possible to see the promulgation of this law as a short-term expedient; a cynical exercise by the centrist-right in heading off the far-right and claiming its clothes. More worryingly, the articles in ML that appear indirectly to support this law smack of the pernicious and racist ideology known as 'Islamaphobia'. Islamaphobia, like any racist ideology, thrives on stereotypical worldviews that seek to dehumanise the *other*, to emphasise their 'backwardness', create negative mythologies and reinforce common misunderstandings.[39] Islamaphobia creates a climate of fear in which every young Muslim is a potential 'terrorist', helping to justify the oppression of minorities by the state. Thus, historical archetypes and contemporary stereotypes of a distinctly Eurocentric character are combined with devastating force to further marginalize the many Muslims who simultaneously have to contend with the effects of economic and social marginalization in European societies. Within the context of growing violence towards Muslims and the progressive curtailment of their liberties in many European countries, it ill behoves anarchists to act as cheerleaders for these developments, or indeed, those states that are acting so repressively. Furthermore, Islamaphobia operates simultaneously at a number of levels – local, national and international – and finds its ultimate expression in a burgeoning American hegemony which seeks to convince us all that the Muslim world is a threat to the peace and stability of the world.

RETHINKING THE UNTHINKABLE

Gemie suggests that 'the first duty of anarchists is that of solidarity with the victims of this repressive wave' and this sentiment is laudable. However, if this solidarity is to be anything other than empty words it must be accompanied by action. In the face of the overwhelming forces arrayed against the principle of liberty this necessarily entails creating broad alliances. As Welsh and Purkis argue it requires anarchists to both recognise and cultivate 'different sensibilities'.[40] As the activities of the Stop the War Coalition in the UK and the creation of new parties such as Respect demonstrate, progressive movements can include many varieties of thought and beliefs. I suggest that anarchism must re-examine its relationship towards religion and those individuals who hold religious beliefs. It is not enough simplistically to reiterate the anti-clerical dogmas of the past. It is not enough, as some contributors to ML have done, merely to consign religion to the status of a 'lie' or a 'disease'. It is not enough to consign Muslims to the category of the duped and write them off as unworthy of any serious consideration.[41]

Despite the rhetoric of anti-clericalism that infused classical anarchism, one can also find many examples of religious thought informing the development of anarchist thought. Moreover, there are some elements of Muslim life which are not completely inimical to anarchism. Indeed, in a twenty-first century Europe dominated by the logic of the marketplace, where we are all encouraged to find our species-being in the fetishism of commodities and the lacunae of consumerism, fashion, celebrity and the mindless pursuit of the superficial, then the anti-materialist stance of Islam is at least worthy of some consideration.[42]

I should stress that I am *not* cheerleading for religion but I am suggesting that anarchists need to be more sensitive to nuances of context and be prepared to make broad alliances in agitation. Within the current climate of state sponsored Islamaphobia, there are opportunities for anarchists to engage *with* Muslims. Perhaps, the readers of ML might better employ their talents through focussed engagement with the young people of Clichy-sous-Bois and Seine-Saint-Denis.[43] As the current disturbances in the *banlieues* illustrate, it is becoming abundantly clear that the French state has failed in its assimilationist and integrationist policies. It has succeeded only in presiding over a situation of growing social divisions, where ethnic minorities are twice as likely to be unemployed and where French Muslims are denied the right to wear the veil in school and where, as a consequence of insensitive (and sometimes brutal) policing, ethnic tensions have now spilled over into violence on the streets.

Some of the readers of ML may argue that these disturbances are fuelled entirely by economic factors or perhaps merely by boredom, and that religion and the banning of the veil has no relevance here. The rioters have been consistently characterized as little more than hooligans, lacking any coherent ideology, but as the correspondent Charles Bremner notes, this is to misunderstand the situation. He writes that,

A street version of radical Islam permeates the youth culture of the estates, where Osama bin Laden is a hero, George Bush and Israel are evil and President Chirac's state wants to stifle their religion and identity by banning Muslim headscarves in schools. The young wreckers refer to one another as brothers and they cite the 'disrespect' of the state for their religion as part of the origin of their revolt.[44]

This suggests that a big part of the current problems in France is the state's refusal to recognise ethnic and religious identities and their place in the lives of individuals and communities; the failure, in the name of *laïcité*, to accommodate cultural difference. Instead, everything is subsumed under the rubric of assimilation and integration into the essentially artificial categories of 'nation' 'republic' and of 'universal citizenship', with all that that implies in terms of the refusal to consider any life outside of the all-embracing arms of the State. Consider an alternative where, in Noam Chomsky's words, we might see hope

> in the capacity of ordinary people to construct for themselves a world suited to their inner needs ... to discover through their own thought and engagement the institutional arrangements that can best satisfy their deeply rooted striving for freedom, justice, compassion and solidarity, at a particular historical moment.[45]

In the final analysis, as Gemie argues, anarchists need to consider seriously which side of the fence they are on – do they support state repression or do they express solidarity with the oppressed?

NOTES

1. Jocelyne Cesari, 'Mosque Conflicts in European Cities', *Journal of Ethnic and Racial Studies* 37:6 (2005) pp. 1015-1024.
2. For example, ten years ago this figure was estimated at 6 million. These figures do not include statistics relating to illegal immigration. Grace Davie, *Religion in Modern Europe* Oxford: Oxford University Press, (2000) p.13.
3. *Ibid.*
4. For a flavour of current debates of the former see Welsh and Purkis, 'Redefining anarchism for the twenty-first century', *Anarchist Studies* 11:1 (2003), pp. 5-12. Chesters, 'Shape shifting: civil society, complexity and social movements', *ibid*: 42-65. Also, responses in *Anarchist Studies* 12:2.
5. My own experiences in the Stop the War Coalition, which has a very broad base that incorporates religious and secular individuals and groups, has informed my thinking here.
6. Paul Chambers, 'Contentious Headscarves: the state and the regulation of spirituality in the twenty-first century', unpublished paper presented at the British Sociological Association's Sociology of Religion Study Group Conference, Bristol 1st April 2004.
7. Anarchists being among some of the most enthusiastic tormenters of the clergy in the 1936 Spanish Revolution.

8. Mikhail Bakunin, *Marxism, Freedom and the State*, London, Freedom Press (1950). http://flag.blackened-net/daver/anarchism/bakunin/marxnfree.html Also see, Mikhail Bakunin, *God and the State*, New York: Mother Earth publishing Association (1916) – available on the web at – http://flag.blackened.net/daver/anarchism/bakunin/gas.html.

9. Interestingly, and in the context of the current discourses in ML, Bakunin states that every people 'has the right to be itself and no one is entitled to impose its costume, its customs, its language, its opinions or its laws.' Quoted in Daniel Guerin, *Anarchism* New York: Monthly Review Press, (1970) p. 68).

10. Errico Malatesta, *Anarchy*, London: Freedom Press (1995: 21).

11. Rudolf Rocker, *Anarcho-Syndicalism: Theory and Practice,* Edinburgh: AK Press (2004) pp. 3-4.

12. I think that this trend is best illustrated in the works of Gerrard Winstanley. See, *The True Levellers Standard Advanced: Or, The State of Community Opened, and Presented to the Sons of Men,* in, George. H. Sabine (ed.) *The Works of Gerrard Winstanley*, New York: Russell & Russell (1965) pp. 247-66. For a useful overview see, Donald R. Sutherland, ' The Religion of Gerrard Winstanley and Digger Communism', *Essays in History* (33) 1990-91, Charlottsville: Corcoran Department of History at the University of Virginia – also available at http://etext.lib.virginia.edu.journals/EH/EH33/suther33.html.

13. David McLellan (ed.) *Karl Marx: Selected Writings*, Oxford: Open University Press (1977) pp. 39-62.

14. Otto Maduro, 'New Marxist Approaches to the Relative Autonomy of Religion. *Sociological Analysis* 1:4 (1977) pp. 359-367.

15. For example, in terms of proto-communist ideas see Christopher Hill, *The World Turned Upside Down: Radical Ideas during the English Revolution*, Harmondsworth: Penguin (1991).

16. Religious heresy being no less 'religious' than orthodoxy. For example, the English civil war saw its genesis in ideas about religious liberty – which then swiftly moved on to a focus on economic & political freedoms – the ultimate failure of the revolution lies in the fact that it was captured by the bourgeoisie. As Hill has consistently argued, it would be a mistake to view something such as the levelling tradition as something 'other' than religion, *ibid*. There are also suggestive parallels with Russia, notably the *raskolnik* tradition of the seventeenth century. These religious dissidents (roughly analogous to the Diggers and Levellers in Britain) were simultaneously religious and anti-state and anti-state religion. Their example was later to influence the *narodnik* movement. See, Victor Postnikov, 'Russian Roots: From populism to radical ecological thought', *Anarchist Studies* 12:1 (2004) pp. 60-71.

17. See, Christopher Hill, *Liberty Against the Law*, London: Allen Lane, (1996). Tom Vague, *King Mob Echo: from Gordon Riots To Situationists & Sex Pistols,* London: Dark Star (2000).

18. See, Paul Chambers, 'Social Networks and Religious Identity: An Historical Example From Wales' in Grace Davie, Linda Woodhead and Paul Heelas (eds.), *Predicting Religion: Christian, Secular and Alternative Futures*, Aldershot: Ashgate (2004) pp. 74-85. Also, Paul Chambers, 'Religion, Identity and Change in Contemporary Wales', in Simon Coleman and Peter Collins (eds) *Religion, Identity and Change; British Perspectives on Global Transformations*, Aldershot: Ashgate (2004) pp. 69-83.

19. William Lambert, 'Some working class attitudes towards organized religion in nineteenth-century Wales' in Gerald Parsons (ed.) *Religion in Victorian Britain – Interpretations,* Manchester: Manchester University Press (1988) pp. 96 -114.

20. Pat Molloy, *And They Blessed Rebecca: an account of the Welsh Toll-Gate Riots 1839 – 1844,* Llandysul: Gomer (1983).

21. See, Trevor Herbert and Gareth Elwyn Jones (eds.) *People and Protest: Wales 1815 – 1880,* Cardiff: University of Wales Press (1990). Also, Gwyn Alf Williams, *When Was Wales?* Harmondsworth: Penguin (1985) and Mathew Cragoe, *Culture, Politics and National Identity in Wales 1832-1836,* Oxford: Oxford University Press (2004).

22. Keith Davies, *The Influence of Syndicalism and Industrial Unionism in the South Wales Coalfield 1898-1921: A Study in Ideology and Practice.* Unpublished University of Wales, Cardiff, Ph.D. thesis (1991).

23. Arthur Horner, cited in Robert Pope, *Building Jerusalem: Nonconformity, Socialism and the Social Question in Wales, 1906-1939,* Cardiff: University of Wales Press, (1998) p. 98. Both Horner and Idris Cox were noted agitators and political theorists who had begun their careers in the chapels but who later rejected religion.

24. Big Bill Haywood, *Bill Haywood's Book: the autobiography of Big Bill Haywood,* New York: International Publishers (1929).

25. Keith Davies, 'Roughneck in the Rhondda: Some ideological connections between the United States and the South Wales Coalfield 1900 – 1914', *Llafur: Journal of Welsh labour History* 6:4 (1995) pp.80-92.

26. Pope, *ibid*: p. 98.

27. The fullest account of these events and processes from the standpoint of religious groups can be found in Robert Pope, *ibid.* See also, Robert Stradling, *Wales and the Spanish Civil War: the dragon's dearest cause?* Cardiff: University of Wales Press (2004).

28. Pope, *ibid*: pp. 6-22.

29. For a fairly comprehensive discussion of these issues see, Steve Bruce, *Politics and Religion,* Oxford: Polity Press (2003).

30. Harold Barclay, 'Islam, Muslim Societies and Anarchy', *Anarchist Studies* 10:2 (2002) pp. 105-118.

31. See, Max Weber, *the Sociology of Religion,* Boston: Beacon Press (1993) pp. 46-59.

32. There are two major theological traditions, *Sunni* and *Shia.* The major schools of thought associated with the former are *Hanafi, Maliki, Shafi* and *Hanbali* – the latter is represented by *Jaffari Fikh.* All these schools of thought are variations on *fikh* (Muslim religious law) and they also have numerous sub-divisions. See, Ahmed Andrews, 'Muslim Women in a Western European society: Gujarati Muslim Women in Leicester' in John Fulton and Peter Gee (eds.) *Religion in Contemporary Europe,* Lampeter: Edwin Mellen (1994) pp. 78-92.

33. I should stress that this is the *ideal.* In practice, one can find many examples of dogmatic forms of Islam. The point that I wish to make is the same as Gemie's – that 'one impulse within Islam was an attempt to create a non-hierchical religion'. Islam can only be understood in terms of that tension between dogmatic and democratic impulses.

34. Weber, *ibid* (262-266).

35. Andrews, *ibid*.

36. Ruqaiyyah Waris Maqsood, *Islam*, London: Hodder and Stoughton (2003). Malise Ruthven, *Islam; a very short introduction*, Oxford: Oxford University Press (1997). Maqsood, I should point out, is a woman and the author of 40 articles and books on Islam.

37. M. Ruthven, *Ibid*, pp. 108 – 111.

38. For example see the work of Kim Knott. A good place to start is 'The Changing Character of the Religions Of Ethnic Minorities of Asian Origin in Britain; final report of the Leverhulme Project' *Community Religions Project Research Papers* (11) Leeds: University of Leeds (1992).

39. Runnymede Trust, *Islamaphobia: A Challenge For Us All*, London: Runnymede Trust (1997). See also, Christopher Allen, 'Endemically European or a European Epidemic? Islamaphobia in a post 9/11 Europe' in Ron Geaves, Theodore Gabriel, Yvonne Haddad & Jane Idleman Smith (eds.) *Islam and the West Post 9/11*, Aldershot: Ashgate (2004) pp. 130-145.

40. Allen, *ibid*, p.7.

41. Stuart Hall's work is illuminating in this respect. Hall, a Gramscian Marxist, argues that under certain conditions 'religious' organization can cement social alliances, provide points of difference, and form the basis of progressive political action. He writes; 'Religious ideologies are *both* the medium in which collective social solidarities are constructed *and* the means through which ideological conflict and difference is pursued. Ideology has its own way of operating and is not simply "the economy" or some other such "reality" merely assuming the false disguise of religious ideas.' Stuart Hall, 'Religious ideologies and social movements in Jamaica' in Robert Bocock and Kenneth Thompson (eds.) *Religion and Ideology*, Manchester: Manchester University Press (1985) pp. 269-296.

42. Conversely, Muslims may find much food for thought in anarchist philosophy. It is becoming increasingly clear that the imposition of western models of 'democracy' based upon the principle of the nation state and rule by elites have been a disaster for Muslims globally.

43. This is not so far fetched as it sounds. As a young man who found himself homeless on the streets of London and surviving through petty larceny, my political education began in 1969 when situationist anarchists aligned themselves with our outcast community of the unwashed and unwanted, introducing us to the basic principles of anarchism and assisting us to organise ourselves into the London Street Commune. For information on the English section of the Situationist International, King Mob, the role of Phil Cohen ('Dr John'), the London Street Commune, the squat at 144 Piccadilly, and the Angry Brigade, see Vague, *ibid*, pp. 43-59.

44. Charles Bremner, 'Go home in the name of Allah, order imams with megaphones', *The Times* (Tuesday November 8th 2005, p. 7).

45. To be found in the preface to Rudolph Rocker, *Anarcho-Syndicalism* (1989) p. iii.

An Immigrant in France: trying to understand the headscarf

TOM CAHILL

Out of the blue, I got an email asking me if I would like to comment on Sharif's article. I suppose Sharif remembered that during the last four years (while I have been trying to make a new immigrant life in France), I have been wrestling a bit with various peculiarities of my new 'homeland'. One of those peculiarities was the complex of issues that arose out of the *foulard* episode he describes (a few hundred French schoolgirls wearing a headscarf in school, plus a few older female state employees). Of course, like all sensitive, postmodern thinkers, I could not possibly attribute, in good conscience, the notion of 'The French' to such a diverse and differentiated group of people. But I admit that I do have the tendency to do just that. Forgive me, differentiators.

This is a short summary of my attempt as a legal, literate, white, European immigrant to learn about French racism, attitudes toward rationality and the Enlightenment, the idea of *laïcité*, the centuries old struggle between the Catholic Church and the Republic, Islam (French and non-French of course), poverty, what they call *communautarisme*, immigration, the meaning of the French Republic, and how the French see 'sects' and other religions in general. Not forgetting capitalism and Europe, of course. All that learning has taken place in the context of where I actually live, what I managed to read and the people I talked to. This is NOT a representative or learned understanding at all. I am still struggling and still don't know all I need to know, much less understand it. I must also warn you that some of my technical details might be just plain wrong. Even highly educated French people, when asked to solve my technical dilemmas or fill in my ignorance, often don't know or disagree. But as a former somewhat anarchist intellectual, I write what I write how I write it. Keep your eyes open for simplifications, even though I know it's all very complicated. I am not paid to write, and have no academic constituency to serve, so I will ignore some complexities and bring others in, so you know that I know that it's a complicated set of issues or problems.

WHAT IS A FOULARD?

More or less suddenly, a year or so after I arrived to France, the *foulard* (the headscarf), sprang into the headlines (although the issue has a previous history). Sometimes, people called it the veil (*le voile*), which I discovered is really not accurate and, to some extent, is even a bit of a 'loaded' way to refer to the simple headscarf. The *foulard* issue was not entirely about the headscarf as such, but clothing research becomes imperative with this issue. Early on I discovered that *hijab* has more than one technical meaning. It is, for example, the general tendency or rule or habit for Muslim women to dress modestly (en.wikipedia.org/wiki/Hijab). It can be merely the modest dressing, not a particular bit of clothing. So any woman can leave her hair uncovered, but the next step up is the headscarf, what my Bulgarian mum used to call a *babushka*. Many (most?) French Muslim women wear no headgear at all in France, except when it is cold. Confusingly, you can also wear a *hijab* which is a headscarf that covers up all your hair and your shoulders, but not your face. Like nuns wear. So the word *hijab* can be used in both ways. You can also have a proper veil (*un voile*), which covers some parts of your face. One could also wear an even more radical garment that covers up every part of your body, except your eyes, ankles and hands. And in the most extreme cases, even the woman's eyes have to see through a kind of mesh. But let us remember that this actual contemporary French episode was about the *foulard*, the simple headscarf, as worn by a few young schoolgirls. Some of those girls wore the *hijab*, the extreme headscarf. That's what started the whole thing and, however the final law was written, that's what it was about in the smallest detail. People often called it the veil (*le voile*) to make it seem like a more heavyweight or radical clothing issue. A fully 'veiled' woman's face is way more bothersome to most people in France (or the part I know about) than a woman with a headscarf. How do you take ID pictures or know who someone is? They could be anyone, even a man! Headscarves are well known in French traditions and it is unremarkable for white French Catholic women wear them. Certainly old French country-women have and do wear headscarves. In fact, until recently, it was considered correct and required conduct for any woman to wear a head covering when entering a Catholic church. Men, on the other hand, had to uncover their hair, and still do.

So pretty quickly, I think I got the basic clothing issues right, but the commentators often confused things. The main fashion point is that the head-scarf is no big deal in terms of radical dress, but this is not how most French people I know see it. For the French (left and right alike), the wearing of the headscarf tends to mean that the schoolgirls who wear it are 'oppressed Muslim women' who are bringing 'religion' into a 'public space', where it definitely does not belong. I am forced to mention here, although it may be obvious, that nearly all of the French and non-French headscarf-wearing women we are concerned with are brown or black. But remember that nearly all of those young women are actually legally French as well. It gets complicated really fast.

WHO WEARS THE *FOULARD*?

The next step of my enquiry was to find out exactly who, in contemporary French society, wore the *foulard* and why they thought they wore this small cloth head garment. As an immigrant without detailed knowledge of French life, this was not completely obvious to me. At first I thought it was probably oppressed Muslim women whose menfolk or Imam more or less forced them to wear at least a headscarf. On the surface, and for most left/alternative inclined people, wearing a *foulard* was a sign of women's oppression. *Voilà!* No more to be said. As usual, I found out it was more complicated than a simple 'oppressed woman' analysis. Although I did get the impression that *most* women wearing the *foulard* were indeed oppressed older women whose men-folk did force them to wear it (or at least that they were women who had always worn a *foulard* and would not think of dispensing with it) I actually know very little about how older Muslim women see the *foulard*. Did any other women wear a *foulard* or start to wear a *foulard*? Were there any other reasons or motivations for wearing it or taking up the practice? It turned out that younger women (at least) wear them for various reasons. Some wear a *foulard* because their parents force them to. That is, the young lasses see no way to disobey orders or defy tradition and practice. Confronted by this situation, some women rebel and refuse to wear the headscarf, though probably not that many (one would have to be very strong, and very supported from outside your family and community to actually rebel radically). So some women refuse to wear them as a rebellion against their parents and/or traditional or strong interpretations of the Muslim duties of a woman.

Digging a bit deeper I found the odd, slightly contradictory fact that some women *wear* them as a sign of rebellion or maybe 'a quest for identity'. They find that they are not able to identify with the kind of non-religious, non-Islamic parents who had attempted to integrate themselves into the French world. They found that they preferred the community of Muslims to 'not belonging' to the 'French nation', even though they ARE French. In other words, put off, angered or depressed by the widely acknowledged difficulties for not-white French in France, they sought support and community 'with their own kind', that is Muslims or persons of colour or both. It is obvious to all that there is still racism and anti-Muslim feeling all over France, so it is equally obvious that a young, brown-skinned, Muslim woman could feel an 'outsider' in French society. We must recall that is logically impossible for a French citizen not to be 'French', and not to be treated 'equally' by the state. All citizens of the *République* are, by definition and understanding of the political elite, treated equally. Even though everyone knows this is nonsense. Sometimes the first generation of immigrants (the parents of some of the young women) tried very hard to be French, and gave up some of the 'old ways'. So there are plenty of actual immigrants who have adapted to and sworn allegiance to the French way. Many of them became French citizens. Those 'integrated immigrants' have left behind the old religious or community-based symbols of identity. The young lasses *choose* the 'traditional community' and clothing that accompanies it for genuine support and a more satisfying identity.

Still other young French women who live in what are called 'difficult or sensitive' areas, wear the scarf for protection. If they don't wear the scarf they will be hassled by the young men that live around them. Seriously sexist behaviour has not vanished in France. Girls with uncovered hair can often be considered a bit 'beyond the Pale', and subject to more hassles, even injury or death, than a 'good Muslim girl'. Some of the macho thugs who live in the high-rise suburbs actually make distinctions as to who they rip off or hassle. Young lad thugs are the same no matter what country or colour or religion. So although wearing the *foulard* might have little to do with any strong cultural or religious identification, it is good protection in a particular neighbourhood.

It's easy to discover the complexity concerning who actually wears the *foulard*. It's less easy to find out how many young lasses who have these different motivations for wearing it live in France at this moment. No one has ever asked. But the variety exists. So you can understand why I often got a bit impatient with a standard simplistic left or anarchist analysis that said that all women who wear the *foulard* are oppressed by their menfolk or by Islam.

CHURCH AND STATE

Sharif has already summed up the basic outlines of the overall problem, so I don't have to repeat it in detail. Because the French 'people/state' had a long and bitter battle with 'religion' (very specifically the Catholic Church), people get really worked up about religion mixing with the 'state' or public life. Usually when commentators refer to 'public life or space', they mean space that is formally controlled by some form of state. What they mean in this context is the schools and the state bureaucracies. The clothing rules (don't wear a *foulard*) do not apply to walking around the streets or going to movies or *médiatheques* (public libraries), or even for people who enter the state bureaucracies as customers. You can also walk around the streets wearing a yarmulke, or a huge cross, or a necklace with a Star of David (all forbidden under the new law in some public spaces). So the new law only applies to a very narrow definition of 'public' space. Many people think pavements and libraries are public space, for example. They also know that many other forms of behaviour are forbidden or state regulated in 'public space', like having a political demonstration.

Technically, and proudly, the French Republic formally allows any religion to be practised in France. There is no state religion. The French (I mean the white intellectual political elite who fought on the side of the state and the Enlightenment, against the Catholic Church and its deep reaching power in pre-twentieth century French society) believe they have separated the church and the state, and done so better than any political culture in human history. The French also see themselves as the true bearers of the wisdom of the Enlightenment. As a result of this long struggle against the Catholic Church, as well as their incredible worship of the Enlightenment and science, the

French state and French intellectuals of all persuasions get really excited about 'cults', which can be anything New Age. In fact, the stubbornly non-religious nature of the French political sensibility gets a little tedious after a while. (Having beaten back the Catholic Church, through a long and bitter struggle, they are not going to let one single gram of religion creep back into precious public space – as the next invasion might be even worse than Catholicism. You can imagine how traditional anarchists, with their strong objection to any form of religion, can easily go along with this).

When confronted by a full-blown religion, embodied in actual Islamic people, who are *also* 'French', things get complex and difficult immediately. Sometimes I get grumpy and mutter about how they 'picked on' the young girls rather than more organised adult Muslims. I wondered what would have happened if they had picked on Muslim women or men in other public spaces, especially since there are many varieties of Islam, some that mix the public and private significantly more than the French. In 'Islamic states' the mix is pretty much complete. It became quite clear to me that this politico/religious history gets tangled up in the seemingly trivial problem of a few schoolgirls who would not take off their headscarf at the school gate. It does mean that you have to understand French history, and especially Republic vs. Church battles during the nineteenth century. Nearly everyone I talked to implied that it was unlikely, not being French, that I would ever really understand this subject and be able to make a judgement. To some extent they are right.

LAÏCITÉ

Laïcité is the key concept in the very extreme, or in any case different, French ideas about church and state. I was quickly reminded that the word did not mean 'secular' – it was more complicated and more French. Sometimes language and culture are like that, so I started looking around a bit. I found out that even though the French say they separate the church and the state (closely related to *laïcité*), they don't actually do it as one might expect (especially if one is 'Anglo-Saxon'). In other words, what seems 'separation' to one person does not seem all that separate to another. For example, I was confused by the fact that all churches constructed before 1905 became the property of the state, as part of the arrangement when the state triumphed over the church. The state took over ownership and responsibility for upkeep of the 'heritage' of all France. Nearly all the churches that were the 'heritage of the French People' were, as it happens, Catholic. To me, if all the infrastructure of the church is taken care of by the state, this means they are intertwined political and economically. It does not mean they are separate. For the French, since all churches are treated the same, and owned by the state, then they are separate (although the state does not own the Tibetan Buddhist monastery and centre near where I live). In some cases, city governments (very much the state in

France) are building mosques for Muslims. Apparently it's the job of the state to 'subsidise' some religions in some ways. I won't go into the complex question of Catholic schools, which also are paid for by the state. In addition, I admit I am not fully sorted about how the state is going to fund a training for truly 'French' Imams. Nearly all of the Imams in France are foreign-trained. The problem is that some of these Imams, trained in (and funded by) the full blown ways of, say, the Saudi Arabian tradition, turn out to be grossly un-adapted to the ways of the French state, the huge majority of French people and even their own flock. Some of the Imams not only don't speak French, but inhabit pre-eighteenth century cultures. This comment is NOT anti-Islam, it is merely a description of the complexity of French Islamic reality. The French State wants to facilitate the French training of Imams so they all are 'Republican Muslims' instead of Saudi Arabian Muslims. These various puzzling details led me think that the French idea of *laïcité*, or separating the church and the state, is not obvious to a non-French person. Although they assure me *'c'est logique'*, when you understand the French people and French history. The point of this *laïcité* is to create a 'neutral public space' free of the influence of religion (read Catholic Church and now add Islam) and a place where the values of the Enlightenment can prosper and grow freely.

WHAT KIND OF RELIGION IS ISLAM?

To remedy my moderately colossal ignorance about Islam itself, I had to do a bit more work. Considering all the fuss, I found that Islam was a regular, standard religion. Islamic leaders all over the world are and have been telling people what the correct path was, what they should do in daily and public life. Quite normal for a religion. Islam did not seem to have an obvious central boss or spiritual leader, like Tibetan Buddhism or Catholicism seem to have. Even in one country there might be conflicts focussed on religious influence and power, *between* various Muslims. One knows who is THE chief as in some religions, like the Archbishop of Canterbury is the chief of the Anglican Church. Islam seems to have fragmented, not only in response to our frag-mented times, but ever since Mohammed died. I guess, at least during the last decade, we have all learned something about Sunnis and Shiites, Wahabists and Tariq Ramadan. Islam, not unlike Christianity and other religions, frag-mented somewhat after the original teacher died, and the conflicts or tensions still exist and mutate.

Fairly quickly, it also became clear that Islam transformed itself slightly wherever it landed. It was flexible in relation to the surrounding and evolving political culture. So you would not and should not expect 'French' Muslims to be exactly like Indonesian, Algerian, Malian or Saudi Arabian Muslims. I also discovered that, like many other religions, there had been a fair bit of Islamic violence, some of it plain vanilla imperialist violence of the conquest type.

Muslims were not peaceful like Quakers or most Buddhists, but more like quite a few Christians. Peace and war in various measures. I don't know enough to rank Islam on a world historical scale, but it seems to be at least as violent as Christianity, maybe more, maybe less.

As with nearly all religions, the patriarchal style and structure seems to be very deep rooted. However, it appeared that the patriarchal tendency in Islam varied a bit, depending on the culture it encountered or in which it was embedded. I should add here that some 'Islamic rules' that apply to women in many Islamic cultures today are, to my sensibility, totally barbaric and unacceptable for anyone whatsoever. Some of these apparently 'Islamic' practices should not be accepted in France today, or anywhere. Although what exactly is 'Islamic' and what is rooted in other aspects of traditional culture is always a bit tricky. One of the crucial aspects in the struggle between the French state and 'Islam' is the battle to force 'Muslims' to treat women at least as well as 'the French' do. My overall impression is that searching for the meaning of 'liberation', for a woman, might be particularly difficult these days in most Muslim religious/political cultures. But the women still struggle!

The degree of interrelation of 'church and state' in Islam seems to vary a fair bit. I found some of the versions of Islam quite easy to handle, as religions go, not all that odd. Some of the Islamic thinkers I read, like Tariq Ramadan, sound very intelligent, critical and progressive to me. I have never been to his supposedly wild-eyed radical lectures, in Arabic, to young Muslims in France. I know that he once made a huge blunder on national TV, getting suckered by Nicolas 'Bully Boy' Sarkozy into NOT condemning outright the stoning to death of women for the crime of adultery. What I am trying to say is that Islam turned out to be a normal patriarchal, quite varied religious system, fighting for market share in a globalised world of consumption and production. The details are always fascinating and different, but the story is pretty much the same.

Of course there were the nutters and really sad extremists. They were very similar to, and as dangerous as, right-wing, military minded, fundamentalist Christians. For example, the blending of an astoundingly patriarchal, Arab culture to a particular serious version of Islam (Wahabism) yields Saudi Arabia. This country is, in my view, one of the most downright despotic and oppressive countries people have invented. So I would never defend Islam as the best example of religion today, and although I sometimes praise some Buddhist practices, I never praise Islam. In fact, to be brutal, I am quite critical of nearly every 'religion' I have ever met. But the result of my enquiry, not deeply surprising, is that Islam is a complicated, fragmented, historically varied, religious practice. People who treat is as a monolith should be told they are wrong, just plain wrong.

I don't know if the progressive, pro-women, reformist, Europeanising tendency in Islam is winning or losing in France. If it is winning, then there is hope for some kind of serious relationship between the French Republican state and French Muslim culture. If the nutter-extremist fundamentalist Muslims are taking the lead, there is going to trouble ahead for many years. Make no mistake, at present it is Islam that has to change, the French refuse. They want to remain French, which means *laïcité* and the accompanying ideology I am outlining here. They know they were in France first and that they have the power. If the 'other' wants to live in France, they cannot remain 'other', they must become 'French'. Some people say this is racist or xenophobic. Some people say that the 'Anglo-Saxon multicultural model' is not for France. These French people are from the left and the right. Just as the new challenge to the 'French way of life' is complicated, so the response to that challenge is complicated.

FRENCH IDENTITY AND 'COMMUNAUTARISME'

During my quest for understanding, I also found it odd that there were no other permissible identities in France other than just plain vanilla 'French'. One can be 'from' somewhere, one can have a family of immense dimensions, once can be a member of an association, but the French state really does prefer that there be nothing much between the individual citizen and the state. No complications. No ethnic identity, no public religious practices, nothing *important* in life determined by skin colour or racial, cultural or regional identity, but everyone equal, in a quantitative way. I am simplifying here only slightly. In the altogether suspicious 'Anglo-Saxon' countries, there are Italian-Americans, Mormons, Anglo-Caribbeans, or even Welsh, all peacefully, if sometimes uncomfortably, co-existing in the same state. In France, everyone is French or not-French. The French guardians of the *République* have a powerfully rooted fear of what they call '*communautarisme*'. They do not want to pander to or even recognise genuine subcultures or communities within France. For example, virtually nowhere in all the state bureaucracies did I ever see anything helpful to immigrants written in any language other than French. The *République* knows full well that many of the people coming to their social security offices are immigrants who speak or read French badly or not at all. They are, after all, immigrants from 'somewhere else'. Most immigrants usually speak more languages than the autochthones, but the immigrants might speak or read the local language poorly. This also includes the up to 500,000 English speaking 'immigrants'. I never found even the most basic documentation in English, much less Arabic or other African languages. If any group is not fully and completely French, they are accused of being a 'separate' community, a kind of cancer which if left to grow 'naturally' will eventually destroy the Republic, and possibly the French way of life. 'They' (the many 'not-French' who are legally recognised persons in France, with Republican rights) are responsible for causing one of the greatest contemporary French problems, *communautarisme*.

In France, non-French people don't feel and act, and therefore are simply

NOT plain vanilla French. This applies equally to British, Dutch, Belgian, Spanish, German or North African people, and their families, who live in France legally or illegally. Many British people are illegal immigrants, that is, without all the proper papers and working/living outside the state system of regulation. You don't hear much about the British (or Dutch or German) immigration problem, although it exists, albeit in a different form than the mostly African immigration problem. In France most people think 'immigration' and they automatically think of African-related immigrants. They are pretty much blind to the nature of the Northern European immigration problem. There are, of course, loads more African immigrants and families than there are European immigrants and their families.

HOW MANY OF 'THEM' ARE THERE?

No one knows how many Muslims or Arabs or Africans there are in France. I found this bizarre, especially given the obvious importance of knowing basic information about them. Because the French Republican elite cling to the idea that all French people are *only* French (which makes them equal in law), not 'something else' as well, the national census does not ask ethnic or religious questions. I don't know the details of the census practices of all the other countries on earth, but I imagine many ask about religion or ethnic background (the USA and the UK ask). The French don't. They just don't see it as a legitimate or important piece of data. Perhaps it is even considered dangerous to ask. The French think there is nothing important to be learned by knowing the religion or ethnic origin of a citizen.

In addition, the French state ideology (French Republicanism) cannot admit to treating religions as genuinely different, or the needs of different religious people as different. So they keep things simple by not counting how many Muslims (or members of any religion) or Muslim or African immigrant/descendants there actually are in France. The ruling French therefore cannot use the state census to find out basic facts like where they live, how many have jobs, how poor they are, how educated they are, and so forth. You should begin to notice that no complex report on the French social situation ever gives a *precise* number or percentage for the population of Muslims, Arabs or Africans in any particular part of France (including the recently rambunctious 'suburbs'), or in France as a whole. They are all estimates. The French Republican ideology pretends that once you are born (or become) a French citizen you are treated equally, *automatiquement*. Under the laws of the Republic, one is dealt with regardless of, and totally ignoring, ethnic origins and religion. So it's a kind of grossly exaggerated, logically correct, quantitative extremism. The only problem with this claim of 'equality', in all nation states and certainly in France, is that it is total nonsense. It's just utterly preposterous to suppose that the needs or duties of an old, non-French speaking, Muslim woman in France are the same as, or equal to, a young, male Catholic, born and raised in Lyon. So they pretend they don't know who is Catholic and who is Muslim, who is white and who is not, they just don't ask. That's how they think. Many French people, especially in ruling political positions, are very proud of this ideology and will be loath to give it up. To begin to take seriously the flawed and unsuccessful Anglo-Saxon multicultural model is something 'many French' are very reluctant to even think about.

Non-French readers have to keep in mind that a lot of these conflicts turn around whether a person, a group or a culture could identify itself as *not* being first and foremost (and only?) French. You might not be aware that foreigners, as foreigners, could not form 'associations' (the ubiquitous legal framework used by nearly all groups in France) until 1985. I can tell you that as an Anglo-British citizen living in France, it is virtually (just to protect myself in case someone has made the leap) impossible for someone who is born elsewhere to become 'really French'. Even if one lives here, has a French partner, has kids go to school in France, pays French taxes and speaks French all day long. And furthermore, and most importantly, I (and many other immigrants) don't even WANT to 'become French'. Yet we still think we are entitled to live here equally, and be treated fairly. I think the not entirely dissimilar actual real-life impossibility for most non-white French to become 'really French' is at the bottom of many of the problems concerning the *foulard*.

We are talking about some form of deeply rooted xenophobia, racism or discrimination here, although it is more complex than it might seem. It is so hard clearly and analytically to separate race, culture, poverty and other important variables. There are plenty of French and foreign people who see the problems of riots in France as a 'basically Muslim' problem. A recent *Sunday Times* commentator wrote half a page on the recent riots, and never mentioned the words racism or poverty. It is nearly impossible to avoid noticing that brown and black French people are not often permitted to feel 'really French'. (Although no doubt a few brown or black French people feel they are as 'really French' as a white French person.) It's hard to call, but for me, until nearly every French white person, or at least 90%, believes that a person who 'looks' like they are 'African', and who might even speak with a solid Midi accent, is in fact 'really French', then there will be a problem. I should also add that even the President of France mentions that France has a big problem with racism. I don't know that I remember leaders like Tony Blair or George Bush say out loud, in an important speech, that their countries have a big problem with racism. The French sometimes can call a cat, a cat (as they say), even if they don't know what to do about it.

THE ACTUAL POLITICAL ACTIONS

This brings us back to a group of young schoolgirls who wore the headscarf, for a variety of reasons, being told that they couldn't wear it at school. There were a few not too impressive demonstrations supporting them. There were some pretty dicey Islamic groups in these demonstrations, as well as the young lasses and their supporters. The left and the trade unions, who swell most demonstrations, plus the 30,000 strong Attac *altermondialistes*, plus many of the democratic, human rights people had a great deal of trouble supporting these young women (and their Muslim male supporters). For obvious reasons, as mentioned earlier, supporting separatist, communitarian or religious practices is pretty hard for normal leftists and French Republican types. Some of these people, as individuals, went along to the demos, but the demos failed to begin to make an impression on the political elite. The fault line in French society held, and most of the girls, a few hundred in all of France, took off their *foulards* at the entrance to the schools, and put them on again when they left. There was not much reportage on what happened to any civil servants who had been or wanted to wear *foulards*. I reckon they just stopped wearing them, as the life of 'functionaries' in France is a good one. Good hours, long holidays, great pensions. No need to take big risks. Things have been left pretty much like that, the teachers still having the job of deciding what exactly was a *foulard* and what is just a decorative piece of female headwear. One of the major purposes of the law Sharif refers to was to relieve teachers of this burden by defining things clearly. They failed.

THE REAL PROBLEM

What was the 'real' problem? It was not actually the headscarf worn by a few schoolgirls. The struggle of the working class against the ruling class often ends up, in a particular instance, being about a few pence more on a wage deal and other small side benefits, once the conflict is crammed into the limiting discourses of contemporary political capitalist institutions. The crisis in modern food production, science and capitalism is not about 'mad cows', even though those cows exist. In a similar way the *foulard* issue was not merely about the *foulard*. It was more complicated. Did separation of the church and state mean that the state really should have nothing to say about religious practice and garment wearing, except if it hurt others? Apparently not. A headscarf never hurt anyone. Wearing a headscarf, as such, by a random group of young women, is actually no big deal. Any more than a reversed baseball cap means all that much. Anyone with a certain amount of sense knows that clothing varies. Some young women would never be caught dead in a short skirt and others never in a long one. Some young women have outrageous (for many French people) hairdos, but these were all right. In short, it was the Muslim girls who were not allowed to do what they had been doing and wanted to continue doing in larger numbers. The lawmakers' defence that all religions were banned from overly visible symbols of religion was a smokescreen. I won't go into the silly semantics around what was obvious and overly obvious; legal language is usually for legal types. You could wear a massive Star of

David or cross hidden under your clothes. I guess you can't really wear a small skullcap or a small headscarf on your head. The law was made to stop young Muslim lasses from displaying or revealing their religion by wearing a headscarf and to preserve, as I have outlined above in detail, the values and practices of the *République*, by banning anything religiously meaningful from certain public spaces.

CAN IMMIGRATION BE STOPPED OR CONTROLLED TIGHTLY

Many French people, including the right wing or xenophobic people, and some others, firmly believe that immigration can be controlled in the modern world, that borders can be closed, and that the movement of people in the world, by and large from poor areas to rich areas, can be stopped. They see economic immigration (trying to earn some decent money), asylum, war casualties, and other causes of immigration as something that a government policy can stop. They think that their countries can fill the dirtiest and worst paid jobs entirely with truly local people. They think they can protect their idea of 'traditional French culture' from being affected by immigrants and their families. Those fearful of immigrants are right to say that integrating large numbers of actually different people, with non-indigenous, non-traditional practices that they wish to continue, into a well developed and complicated existing political and cultural system is really hard to do. I don't know that there are many examples of wildly successful 'integration' on earth. In our era, immigration has become rampant throughout the rich world. There are exceptions, like Japan, where massive immigration is less likely. Britain, and especially the USA (who are obviously the global champs as the preferred immigrant destination), began the process of receiving large numbers of immigrants earlier than France. But the French believe that nothing is to be learned from these Anglo-Saxon experiments, which they believe are a complete failure. So anti 'not-French' people (racists or xenophobes?) are right that there is a huge problem trying genuinely to integrate large numbers of immigrants, especially those of a different colour and religion. They are of course wrong, totally wrong, that they can make the problem go away by ultra tight border controls. However, the fences are getting higher and longer throughout Europe.

NEUTRAL PUBLIC SPACE

A word on 'neutral public space'. Some French people think that not only does this neutral public space exist in France, but that the creation of this neutral public space was a direct result of the mix of current French practice in regard to *laïcité*, *communautarisme*, and the wider values of the Republic and the Enlightenment. It's struck me that in the frantic fight against the religious (read Islamic) invasion of public space, many French people have rather neglected a far more serious threat to public space: global capitalism. It is clear enough that the purchase and privatisation of formerly public space, the commodification of space, is far more dangerous and pervasive than the problem of Muslims dressing differently in schools. I remember walking by an insurance agent recently and noticing that the signifying device outside the agency shone down on the pavement as well. If you looked down, on the pavement, quite obviously public space, you saw the logo of the corporation. I wondered if the Mayor of the town had a policy and maybe rented the space. For me the most vital problem comes from commodification, although I don't deny that mixing of religion and politics causes some problems too.

My own experience is that there is not much more 'neutral public space' in France than in the USA or Britain. I would admit that at this point in history there might be a little less public space in America than France, but in my experience there is roughly as much in Britain as in France. My basic contention is that public space is more and more for sale in the world today. More and more private. If you are rich, or know people who are, then you can find a public space to rent or buy anywhere you like. If you are not connected, then you can't find public space so easily. If it is true that France is, for the moment, resisting the globalisation of everything, the commodification of everything, including space, better than elsewhere in Europe, then we should be proud of their resistance. To me it was clear that the recent *NON* on the Euro-referendum demonstrated this resistance, among other things, quite clearly. To some extent, I would expect that, all things considered, there is more uncommodified public space in France than in many other countries. But the difference, on the ground, is not that great, and I would be hard pressed to figure out how you would weigh up this question with any precision.

CONCLUSION

As you can see, in spite of my passionate, amateur, non-comprehensive research, I am still confused a bit by the overall French political elite view of this headscarf matter, much less the related larger issues. I find their notion of *laïcité* both extreme and full of contradictions and tensions. I don't think it is appropriate for the modern world, with unstoppable immigrations of all sorts of people to all sorts of places. I am stunned by the French state's inability to acknowledge that some of their immigrants are not French (for example, don't speak French well, or at all) and to make some sort of effort to spend a bit of money to teach them French. The Germans do. At the very least, they could print a few leaflets for them in their own language, regarding social benefits, rules of behaviour and so forth. As a legal immigrant I found it practically impossible to get any neutral help in English. Think of the poor folk who speak Arabic or a less widely spoken language, especially if they have no family or community to help them. I also think that they have been slightly blinded or obsessed by their historical battle with the Catholic Church, even though the world has moved on.

The French ruling political elite seem to believe that if it says something in the constitution of the Republic, then it must be so. If everyone is an equal citizen of the Republic, then there cannot be and must never be sub-cultures, sub-communities, and religious practices in neutral, open, public spaces. Yet it is obvious there are sub-communities, sub-cultures and religious practices visible all over the place. The equality of treatment of churches means that the massively expensive and ill-attended Catholic churches are never allowed to go into serious disrepair (national heritage after all, and bit of a tourist attraction). The fast growing Muslim population is not well served by fancy mosques or any mosques at all in some places. When all the churches built before 1905 are owned and looked after by the state, then the meaning and practice of 'separation of church and state' is, at the very least, a challenging notion. Furthermore, the denial of the official existence of race or religion as important variables, even though everyone admits that racism and religious practice are a problem, is a strange way to hide what is going on in France today. I think the long-running affair of the *foulard* has shown the tensions, very much unresolved, in French society. Although I have said nothing about the recent riots throughout France, it seems to me rather obvious that those riots have their causes rooted in some of the problems I have mentioned.

One of the most interesting things about my immigration to France is discovering the small and large differences between my previous countries and this one. It is no longer a surprise to me that the French are deeply attached to a doctrine concerning the Enlightenment, race, ethnicity, religion and so forth that is full of tensions and at times still seems quite bizarre, or at any rate, very French. The management of those tensions involves dealing with a particular combination of factors in France. Of course, there are equally complex tensions in other countries. Understanding how the French deal with their contradictions is, nonetheless, a continuing challenge to me, and to the French. But they really should have let those lasses wear the headscarf in school. I was really disappointed that *all* the female students didn't turn up one day with headscarves. Now that *would* have been interesting.

The trial of *Le Monde libertaire*

RONALD CREAGH

The issue of headscarves worn by Muslim schoolgirls in France has been a hot issue since 1989, though the matter came to a head in October 2005. Such an important controversy raises questions about how French anarchists should respond to social movements. Should they cultivate links with the various protagonists? Should they respect minority religions? What type of action or ideology contributes to human emancipation? And in the present case, what positions should be adopted towards state institutions such as *laïcité* and the school system?

Sharif Gemie, examining this event through the articles in *Le Monde Libertaire*, concludes that, both in form and content, anarchists have failed to deal adequately with the situation. Machismo and dogmatism have been used to approve of a repressive state law. Anarchist writers have fallen victim to oversimplification and confusion. They have failed to take into account the schoolgirls' positions and introduced into their arguments references to customs or practices from other countries, irrelevant to the French case.

The issues discussed here have occurred in a broad context, in which at least four broad trends must be taken into account: on one hand, the antireligious campaigns of the past and their historical heritage, (*laïcité*); and the various post-68 movements of emancipation, including the feminist campaigns and dress codes in schools; on the other hand, the ethnic conflicts that accompanied the Algerian War of Independence and their aftermath – large-scale immigration, anti-Arabic xenophobia and the rise of *communautarisme*; and last, but not least, the rising tide of Islamic movements. None of this background can be overlooked when evaluating the matter.

Other important issues, which would require lengthy development are also at stake in this debate. They cannot be discussed within the limits of this paper but ought at least to be mentioned: the slow destruction of the French school system, deliberately organized to prepare its privatization; the difficult dialogue between adults and teenagers; the different perception of adolescence in western culture as compared to other societies; the possibility of an emancipation which does not follow the process of westernization; and, finally the treatment of this debate by various power groups who wish to dominate these populations.[1]

This response is limited in form and content. I cannot reply in the name of the various authors; it is up to them to think about Gemie's remarks. I will also set aside discussion on the way anarchist debates should be conducted, as this would also require a full-length analysis. The present discussion will outline the multidimensional aspects of the issue and, since a fruitful social debate is an exchange, offer answers to Gemie's questions whilst suggesting new lines of inquiry into anarchist conception(s) of public space and the abstract French concept of citizenship.

The first part of this article will clarify the social setting of ML and of the Muslim groups mentioned by Gemie, as well as their relation to 'fundamentalism'. The paper will then deal at greater length with the French concepts of *public space*, as defined in 1905 by the separation of church and state and *laïcité*, established in 1946, two principles which British and American people have never grasped.[2] The headscarf issue will then be presented in the third part of this article. I meet Gemie's outrage at the intrusion into the debate of other forms of female oppression (such as excision or polygamy) with the contention that these are linked with the headscarf legislation and will probably create new conflicts in the near future.[3]

1. READING *LE MONDE LIBERTAIRE*

Sharif Gemie argues that ML express views inherited from an obsolete past, that its writers have ignored the non-religious contexts of the headscarf and wrongly approved the state's repressive law. As one goes through 'The trial of Fatima' it is apparent that Gemie's paper is really 'The trial of *Le Monde Libertaire*'. He accuses the paper of not having sided with the FLN during the Algerian war, and ironically asserts that it is now using the same language as Islamists.

This is indeed quite an accusation, and an implicit assimilation of the anarchist position with the attitude of French colonizers in Algeria, who used to call any housemaid or prostitute by the name 'Fatima'; it implies that *Le Monde Libertaire* similarly oppresses all young Muslim girls who wish to cover their heads since it excludes them from its debates and refuses to recognize that their behaviour might be conducted for non-religious reasons.

The paper is also accused of imagining the mores of Muslims in France, particularly the Arabs, as replicating some of the oppressive practices of other countries. And it exacerbates the confusion by the frequent use of the word 'fundamentalism', a vague term of which the writers seem to be fond.

I shall discuss later the reference to foreign countries and the supposed confusion between heterogeneous customs. Let me first remind the reader of how *Le Monde Libertaire* works and what it generally understands by 'fundamentalism'. I will then discuss the French anarchists' general position on religion and the education issue.

How representative is Le Monde Libertaire?
It should be clear at the outset that if the French weekly is one of the most important in the European movement, the health of the anarchist movement is

rather poor: the French Federation has between two and three hundred activists, and is far from representing the whole range of libertarian opinion.[4] To construct a uniform discourse from a statistical set – 12 articles in two years (5 or 6 in a month and a half) – amounts to eliminating each author's specificities and individual response to the particular circumstances at the time of his or her contribution.

The *Monde libertaire* certainly does not represent any official position of the Federation (FA) even though that organization is the only one to express itself in the paper. But the movement has no professional and specialized journalists, no reporters and no sufficient means to conduct a survey. No editorial agenda is defined beforehand and the authors of articles are unsolicited: the texts are placed as they come, or rather as they trickle in. There is no editing room, but only one person in charge, delegated for a year, assisted by a handful of volunteers.

How does the paper understand 'fundamentalism'? Another anarchist organ Radio libertaire provides a useful clue. On various occasions, Radio libertaire have invited a number of women to speak on the issue (a particularly important communication came from Mimouna Hadjam). These women have given quite detailed and impressive information about the introduction of polygamy among Maghrebian immigrants in France, the immigration of radical Imams, the moral pressures on men and women (and many forms of social intimidation) to exclude young girls from extra-curricular activities organized by public or private associations and place them in Qur'anic schools.[5]

What place for religion?
Gemie considers the anarchist authors of ML as repressive, because they support repressive state legislation and do not listen to the schoolgirls' expression in favour of the headscarf.

Can one consider anarchist argumentation in defence of the law of March 15, 2004 about religious symbols in schools as support for a state limitation of freedom? Indeed, no anarchist would believe that freedom can be granted by the state because emancipation is understood as an individual and collective process. But while state legislation will never emancipate anyone, some laws may be better than others and anarchism does not compel people to oppose systematically any state action.

If the wearing of a headscarf is a purely cultural act, as Gemie generally supposes it to be, can't people other than the schoolgirls concerned have some say in the matter? And what if it is not? Can our friend explain how a Muslim girl can make, as such, a purely cultural choice since Muslims reject the distinction between 'culture' and 'religion'? Islam explains the totality of the world and links every single thing to that totality. It aims to create a religious identity that covers all aspects of life; and Muslim leaders feel threatened by westernization in respect of their religious standpoints, not to defend the variety of their cultures. From the mosque to the halal butcher, religion provides the social link; there is none for the non-Muslim or the atheist Arab. Can Sharif explain where religion ends and where culture starts?[6] Isn't it because there is no such frontier that, in the same text in which he accuses French anarchists of not wanting to see the non-religious context of the head-scarf, he ends by asking them to recognize at least 'the religion of minorities'. Rather than trying to understand the position of French anarchists, in truth our friend invites them to reconsider it. For him, a conception of libertarianism that fails to rehabilitate religion cannot be considered as serious.

The anarchist critique of religion, expressed in the motto 'No God, no Master', is also a clear position against Islam as a religion, not against Muslim populations. The issue is not whether a religion is freely adopted or not: if one thinks that religion alienates the individual and the group, should s/he not fight its influence? Belief is radically different from critical reasoning, because the faithful is not a 'subject' in the philosophical sense, taking a distance from a certain proposition and discussing it. S/he is only an 'ego' who belongs to a group and will not leave it. And a religion that refers to some transcendent entity is the nest of the state because human beings give up their capacity and power to create the world, which they entrust to those people supposedly blessed by that invisible entity, reducing politics to a relation of domination-submission.[7]

Rhetoric and fundamentalism

Let us now look at the supposed similarity between the discourse of ML and that of the Islamists, 'a series of experts who offer contrasting interpretations of accepted principles, relying on their experience, their charisma or the force with which they speak to gain acceptance'. If the use of the same rhetoric creates a similar intellectual or philosophical position, then how can our author say: 'There is no one single Islam' or that there are important differences between Islamist writings. It is true that there are no other forms of address other than those that are grounded on the principles recognized by a community, on the experience of their authors and on their rhetoric. But are these common features a sufficient condition to make all *discourse* alike? Why not examine if 'the appeal to authority' (*argumentum ad verecundiam*) is put forth, and how 'emancipation' is defined by religious people and anarchists respectively?

Anarchists who refer to 'religious fundamentalism' describe a group for which, literally interpreted, religion is the source of law applied to daily life (and therefore does not concede any autonomy to the sphere of culture). Such a collectivity can even be considered as die-hard conservative (*intégriste*) if it refuses to accept that others might have differing interpretations. The Union of Islamic Organizations in France (UOIF), mentioned by Gemie, is indeed fundamentalist and quite inflexible in its opinions. How can one believe that they are indifferent to religious issues? They control several major mosques, and some 300 associations, such as the Young Muslims of France (JMF) and the Muslim Students of France (EMF). Whether one likes it or not, they are also considered to be close to the Muslim Brotherhood. 'The Qur'an is our constitution' declares their president, Lhaj Thami Breze in *Le Parisien* of February 12, 2003, and one of their co-founders, Ahmed Jaballah, has declared: 'The UOIF is a two-story rocket. The first is democratic, the second will put an Islamic society in orbit.'[8]

The limitations of a debate
As in any legislation, the last word belongs to the people, not to the legislator. The role of a schoolteacher is to allow the young to debate those questions that they feel important or stressful. French high schools have courses on sexual reproduction, on the history of beliefs and religions and on the study of cultures. They must avoid biased debates, even if perfect objectivity is never possible. Still, educators must not be forced to remain politically correct by ignoring, for instance, Christian witch-hunts or the stoning of women preached by certain Islamic theologians.[9] In practice, the acceptance of multiculturalism in Great Britain and its rejection in France have had similar outcomes. Laws and proclamations in both countries conceal the harsh reality of racism and xenophobia, the ethnic wars and the collective political performances that do not correspond with the professed beliefs of those responsible for inequality and domination. Let us emancipate one another and leave the deadly games to the specialists in power relations and domination. But to liberate ourselves, must we not fight to protect a public space against the religious quicksand into which it might sink? Should French left libertarians demand religious tolerance and forsake *laïcité*?

2. THE FRENCH CONTEXT: PUBLIC SPACE AND LAÏCITÉ

Laïcité is an outcome of religious conflicts in French history; it is related to the sphere of the state and must not be confused with tolerance and public space. Its roots can be traced to a particular understanding of Enlightenment thought, and the fight against all forms of dogmatic authority. This had two aspects. On the one hand, the French bourgeoisie, following the lead of Voltaire and the *encyclopédistes*, fought to establish a space that opened up the possibility for any belief and unbelief. On the other hand, a popular anticlerical movement contested the ecclesiastic authority of the Catholic Church. Whilst the dispute about religious dogmas that hindered scientific conclusions was largely confined to intellectual circles (the antireligious fight of free thinkers, rationalists and atheists only had a minor impact), anticlericalism spread to a large section of society. And the struggle against the various forms of French Catholic power resulted in the separation of state and church in 1905.

The separation of Church and State

Public services freed themselves from the clergy; for instance, baptism certificates were no longer accepted as official birth certificates. Thus, rather than an antireligious attitude, it was an anticlerical and anti-dogmatic mentality that developed in the population (though people today are rather indifferent to religious practice, particularly since World War II).

The separation of church and state created three different spaces: the private space of individuals and families, the public and social space of civil society (for instance, the street), and the civil and public space of the state. France has indeed two forms of public space: while religion can express itself in the former, it is excluded from the latter because it cannot be used as a form of temporal power on other people.

The space of the state excludes any reference to religion within the power system. Religion has no place in the body politic.[10] This separation between state and church implies that the state is the unique source of legislation and law. It therefore cannot express any position that would favour a metaphysical or religious preference. Any civil servant who displays his or her creed in the exercise of office makes it a public affair and confers the status of official recognition. This is why, for instance, a minister or a member of the state administration (a schoolteacher or a medical doctor in a public institution) cannot display any religious affiliation.

This restiveness towards any tendency to intellectual and, in particular, clerical domination, is apparent in civil matters. There has never been in France a political party openly calling itself 'Christian Democrat'. Even the defunct MRP – a Catholic party – did not dare say so, though it included some priests among the elected members (notably the *chanoine* Kir (1876-1968), mayor of Dijon and member of parliament, who is now only remembered for having given his name to an aperitif).[11]

The same is not true in other countries, for instance the United States, where liberal traditions are held up in opposition to Jacobinism and the concern to treat all citizens as equals in the abstract. Such an abstract, impersonal citizen corresponds indeed to the will of the state to suppress any intermediary body, so as to reign supremely over individuals without resistance.[12] On the other hand, the French consider that *communautarisme* implies factionalism – power struggles between groups – and therefore a certain hierarchy and discrimination; furthermore, it excludes those who reject this tradition or who, like atheists, do not form a community.

Beyond the sphere of the body politic, the situation is quite different. The French state officially recognizes the existence of chaplains in public services (public hospitals, prisons, the army, and schools), and the minister of education sends to all school establishments a list of religious feasts and religious prescriptions of the various denominations. One day a week (Wednesday) pupils are liberated from school obligations in order to allow religious instruction to those who wish to receive it. School lunchrooms must respect a number of culinary instructions, particularly during Ramadan. Last but not least, there is an official recognition of French Catholic tradition: it is Sunday, and not the Sabbath, for instance, which is the official day of rest.

The various denominations have created their own lobbies to enter the power system. Some of them are perfectly visible and officially recognized, others work covertly, for instance the Opus Dei.[13] These links to the power system bring financial returns. The Vichy laws concerning church property have never been rejected. In the year 2002, the socialist Jospin government established a permanent discussion committee between the state and the Catholic Church. In 2005, forty billion euros were given to private schools: that was the equivalent to two-hundred-thousand teaching positions. The *taxe d'apprentissage*, a tax levied as a contribution to state technical training schemes, distributed in 2002 the following sums: €105 per pupil to state schools; €332 per pupil to private establishments under contract; and €1790 per pupil to private establishments that did not have any contract with the state. One should also mention the stipends of the Catholic, Protestant and Jewish ministers in the Alsace-Moselle region, which is still under the regime of a concordat which no one knows anything about outside France. It requires little imagination to see what financial benefits other religious groups might be looking for.

Religious groups increase their domination when they are closely linked with power. In colonial America, Jesuits gave arms to those individual Indians who converted to Christianity. Today, religious leaders seek to modify power by preventing free speech. We are presently witnessing attempts to reintroduce in France a law against blasphemy.[14] Internal clerical pressures against the French separation between religious and political powers are now boosted by external pressures, exerted both by the US government (especially since the French government's criticism of the invasion of Iraq) and the pressure to sign up to the European constitution. France seems more and more isolated in a world where religion is resurgent, appearing as spectacular politics.

The independence of civil society from religious influence (and one might add from economic dogmatisms) is slowly shrinking. The fight against political neutrality has now entered the school system. There have been campaigns to introduce religious teaching within state schools. And political conservatives like Bayrou lead continual attacks against *laïcité*.

Schools and the laïcité principle

The *laïcité* principle is not juridically grounded in the separation of church and state, but it must be understood within that context. It was brought in and fought for by Jews, Protestants and Freemasons, in particular, to protect their rights against the dominant Catholic Church. It may also be seen as a protection for unbelievers and a space of freedom for whoever wants to distance themselves from religious affiliation.

The principle may also be interpreted as a fundamental problem in political philosophy: neutrality means that the state cannot impose its own conception of the good on citizens. Its sole reference is the general will as expressed by the majority.

Laïcité is required in public space whenever it is necessary to maintain security and peacefulness. It is therefore locally modulated according to rules established by the various authorities, for instance municipalities. The street, for instance, remains under the control of the state. Any religious sign can be worn, but anyone who wishes to set a table in the sidewalk to distribute pamphlets or other materials is required to seek authorization. Most anarchists would object to the principle of public security, since it often serves as an excuse to the powers that be.

In contrast with universities, schools have no autonomy and are regulated by the Ministry of Education. As Catherine Kintzler explains, France is a society based not on tolerance but freedom. Tolerance supposes that different groups may coexist; the principle of freedom does not take groups into account because, after all, a citizen may not wish to 'belong' to any group whatever. In practice, tolerance often results in the acceptance of faith, but not in the acceptance of the faithless. It allows other religions to coexist, for reasons I cannot develop here. But it is impatient with people who do not want to belong to a community. And unbelievers do *not* form a community. They appear as a threat to the social link.[15] Furthermore, 'tolerance' today often means that all opinions are respectable and anyone is free to think whatever one likes. This relativism crushes all critical reasoning and can lead only to violence.[16]

To return to education, a different objection comes to mind: don't teenagers have the right to experiment, to make mistakes, to confront themselves on such important issues as sex, politics and religion? A friend tells me that the school that talks only about mathematics is a miserable place. True. But teenagers are not 'free': they are in a process of building their personality and their freedom. This means that schoolchildren are not consumers and that the school is not a social public space of civic society but a social public civic space of the State.

Multiculturalism and group conflicts

How can one defend a multiculturalist viewpoint and deny in the same time a very specific feature of French culture? France is experiencing an ideological battle. If the place of religion in schools is discussed and *laïcité* proves to be a protection, then those who want to remove it should at least suggest an equivalent safeguard. Moreover, those who seek to defend liberal traditions must also take into account the fact that there are in France some 35 thousand victims of forced marriages.[17] As for religion, there is not one Muslim community in France, but many. Some show strong reservations about essential religious duties: 79% of Algerians declare that they do not go to the mosque on Fridays.[18] Yet an atheist Algerian receives no recognition:

the Minister of Interior and French authorities in general hold discussions with religious authorities when they want to settle issues concerning Algerian communities.

Gemie advises anarchists not to 'draw nightmare comparisons from the quite different contexts of Iran or Bangladesh'. Yet differing behaviours also depend on the country of origin. It is not an unnecessary confusion to notice when domestic religious organizations, like everything else, operate under external influences. The Paris Grande Mosque, linked to the Algerian community, is financed by the Algerian government (about €700 000 a year[19]). The Muslim Committee of French Turks (CMTF) depends on the Turkish Foreign Affairs. One could continue this enumeration.

One must also remember that the judgments concerning women (genital mutilation, repudiation, custody of the children, polygamy) pronounced in some African countries are applicable in France, following the agreements passed by the French government with these countries.[20] It thus appears that France, the country of 'the rights of man', does not protect the rights of a woman once they are repudiated by a polygamist, or of a very young girl married to some unknown grey-beard.

These facts contribute to an inexcusable and evident xenophobia or racism among certain segments of the French population, all the more because the country has not just received isolated individuals but experienced a massive and permanent influx of immigrants. Isolated individuals seldom cause any problem anywhere. Large-scale settlements establish an *esprit de corps* and create a certain solidarity which appears somewhat anomalous in a country where 'individualism' is the general practice; furthermore, a conspicuous minority refuses to integrate into the general society, particularly in the school system.

On the French side, the police seem to be the leading edge of ordinary racism: innumerable people are constantly arrested solely on account of their appearance: their African origin. France has always been torn by internal conflicts, in past times between neighbouring villages or different provinces. Today France experiences different, more intense, clashes: for instance, between Arabs and Gypsies and competing religious denominations. Fortunately, 'French people of old stock' no longer have those spells of patriotism which one may observe in other countries, and the three coloured flag is rare on private balconies on July the 14th. Yet the regional wars of a distant past, succeeded by autonomist struggles and long lasting but more superficial animosities, have given way to new religious, ethnic and sexual configurations, previously covert or little known. Thus new forms of domination appear, in the shape of *communautarisme*. It is no accident that women, or French people of North African origins, are hardly represented among the ruling class. And one may also notice the various attitudes that reject the recruitment of certain ethnic groups, ranging from extreme right-wing racists, (grounded in the idea of a genetic inequality of 'races'), to ordinary xenophobes. Thus a new generation has, in its turn, re-opened the debate and stirred up controversy resulting in a law which forbids 'ostentatious' religious signs, and particularly the veil or foulard (which the media present as 'Islamic'). Such legislation costs the state nothing and it distracts citizens from their more essential demands. They substitute internal class strife for social struggle against economic subjection. Ethnic conflicts are a godsend for managers. Internal working-class conflicts prevent all attempts to unify the labour movement in a struggle for its common emancipation.

3. THE STATUS OF THE HEADSCARF

In all times, education establishments have given close attention to the question of pupils' dress. In the 1960s France reacted against boys with long hair and girls wearing miniskirts or tights; sanctions went as far as exclusion. Since May 1968, there has been a growing repugnance towards uniform: it may be that the memory of fascist outfits haunts the collective subconscious. Whatever the case, French state schools abandoned uniform long before many other countries. Only on rare occasions do any of the professions, and particularly the academy, display any distinctive sign. As for the dresses of particular provinces, these now have only a folkloric or a commercial meaning.

The law of 1905, establishing the separation of church and state, forbade the wearing of a crucifix or a kippa in state schools. Many adults today still remember incidents where they or some comrade were called to order for having too openly infringed the rule.

For Sharif Gemie the headscarf has many connotations, and it is simplistic to consider the religious aspect alone. But that is the perspective through which the question was set by the Muslim leaders and by the state, even though it probably conceals other aims of those involved. But since what is at stake is not always explicit, let us satisfy ourselves with examining the nature of the debates, as they occurred publicly.

The position of the French resonates with the country's colonial past. It was during this period that the headscarf was first denounced as a symbol of women's oppression. The French press in the 19th century had already used those terms, particularly about the Algerian colony. But to confuse the colonialist attitude towards the 'Fatimas' with contemporary reactions, expressed by other generations and in a quite another context, amounts to the same mix up as situating the present conflicts in the tradition of the crusades, as some political leaders of the extreme right would claim. Unfortunately, collective decisions are made according to the interpretations people construct to help understand their world. Refusing to see the specificity of a particular situation amounts to taking refuge in a phantasmagorical universe, with disastrous consequences.

The 'voile' issue begins in September 1989, a few months after Ayatollah Khomeini invited all faithful Muslims to execute Salman Rushdie, the author of *The Satanic Verses*. The *fatwa* made the headlines in the French press and created a very negative impression. Not surprisingly, when three schoolgirls refused to remove their headscarves in a high school in the Paris region, Islam became headline news. That very month the board of trustees of the *Conseil français du culte musulman* (CFCM) declared that 'the wearing of the head-scarf is a religious prescription', expressing the strong influence of the National Federation of French Muslims, which is dominated by Moroccans. Thus the story of the 'veil' began life as a religious issue.[21]

In this context, anti-Arab and anti-Muslim xenophobia progressively changed into anti-Islamism.[22] The September 11 attack against the World Trade Centre reinforced this attitude. Indeed it is now difficult to distinguish anti-Islamism from a widespread anti-Arab xenophobia, a result of the post-colonial heritage, class conflicts and internal class strife. Many French tend to think that all Muslims are Arabs, that all Arabs are Muslims, and they confuse conservatives with fundamentalists.[23]

Clashes in educational establishments arose in various areas, and different solutions were adopted, since each high school disciplinary board took independent decisions. On October 11, 2003, the Lycée Henri Wallon, in Aubervilliers, decided to exclude two sisters who insisted on wearing the veil 'to protect their modesty'.[24] Their father (who is Jewish), and a member of the MRAP (Movement against racism and for friendship between people) decided to go to the courts.[25]

Finally, in September 2004, the law was changed: what was now forbidden in schools were symbols that were *ostentatoire* ['ostentatious'] not those that were *ostensible* ['apparent']. Though the difference is not evident at first sight, it is semantically clear: *ostentatoire* has the 'character of what is unavoidably noticed, that is too showy'. In contrast, ostensible refers to what is 'conspicuous, clearly shown'.[26] In practice, the overtones can only be defined by their context, and this leaves grounds for discussion. While the bandanna and the headscarf belong to the French tradition, the *hijab* which goes round the face and covers the shoulders is clearly reminiscent of nuns. As long as it does not become a high fashion trend, it cannot but carry religious connotations.[27]

It is traditional for religious partisans of the headscarf to describe themselves as victims. And it is clear that Muslim communities can consider themselves as oppressed since they have endured all sorts of discriminations, including multiple obstacles against the construction of mosques. But what about the headscarf? If one considers for instance the large demonstration of January 16, 2004 against the legislation on the *foulard*, which brought out some five thousand people in Paris and the provinces, one notices that two groups attracted particular press coverage. The majority was organized by the *Parti des Musulmans de France* (Party of French Muslims), who had called for the demonstration. That organization was founded by Mohamed Enacer Latreche and has political goals. This is the very first time in contemporary

French history that a party has been officially linked to a religious confession. One might also notice its contacts with … the extreme right.[28] The other group included some 200 Indonesians. Their demonstration was not in the name of some ethnic identity but of religion, as it represented the international Islamist movement Hizb-ut-Tahrir, and shouted 'The *hijab* (*foulard*) is obligatory, not an embellishment'.

All this clearly shows that the wearing of an emblem does not get its meaning through the intention of the person who displays it, but through the interpretation given by the various collectivities that come into play. Thus, in the same way as anarchists may well claim that they do not identify with bomb throwers, society as a whole generally rejects that protest and continues to judge them as potentially violent trouble-makers. In the same way, it is the opinion leaders, corporate media and political hacks who decide what part of the body or what attire has a religious meaning. And in so far as the wearing of a veil is considered to be 'religious', its appearance in public schools transforms it into a symbol of religious conflict. This is already the case today in a number of schools or institutions as I have learned from a number of teachers. If we are to believe the testimony of a teacher of the school where a girl shaved her head in protest, the pupils who no longer wear the veil are much more lively and express themselves much more than had previously been the case.[29] If wearing the veil is a sign of submission, at least there are places in France where it is not compulsory.

Everyone has come across a number of situations where some adult women could not be accepted with their heads covered in state establishments. But is it by wearing a scarf that they will come out of their ghettoes? Would most Muslim leaders accept such a situation? The integration of their subordinate women would deprive them of power and income. In any case, the battle for wearing the veil or *foulard* has social impact and introduces the religious sphere into public space, with the resulting risk of suppressing a protection offered by that neutral area.

A French anarchist, the geographer Elisée Reclus, recognized the importance of groups united by a common history, language and territory. Such is not the case of *foulard* bearers, and one may prefer a community freely chosen to the one ascribed by birth. May we not imagine affinity groups variously federated that work for the emancipation of all social movements? One should, of course, avoid essentialist discourses that freeze once and for all 'religion', 'culture' or some particular ethnic group. And this is the case in France where a number of immigrant collectivities have no chance of being considered truly French. One has to avoid the generalities of political discourse: our place as social dissidents is in the micro battles of everyday life against all forms of xenophobia, racism, anti-Semitism, repression, machismo and ethnic patriotism. After all, as anarchists, we know that we too are alienated and have to fight against today's monsters.

I must thank André Bernard, D. H., Yasmine Mouzaoui and Alain Thévenet for all their information and suggestions. Tom Cahill and John Clark reviewed and commented upon a large portion of this article. All have very largely contributed to my present position and argumentation, even though there are major disagreements between us. Of course, I am solely responsible for the mistakes and viewpoints expressed.

NOTES

1. Indeed, the totally inadequate treatment of social issues by state and media generates a cold war climate that reduces all discussion to binary thinking: yes or no answers. It also propagates a vision of insecurity which creates among the settled population some new version of the 'domino theory': people come to imagine that any concession will open the door for new demands and fantasize all sorts of dramatic outcomes. For instance, some people imagine that if scarves were authorized in schools, Arab girls who would reject them might be more vulnerable to aggression.

2. Indeed, *laïcité* is a term with no adequate English equivalent, the word secularism having a broader meaning.

3. Let us not forget what is at the core of the issue. What is at stake is not a piece of cloth, but the schoolgirls who wear it. Yet, though we must pay attention to people, first and foremost, I will not discuss here the schoolgirls' situations, but the veil or scarf issue. There are no pupils or students in general, but individuals who each have their own particular story and their uniqueness. And if we do want to help those groups in the younger generation, let us help them create their own means of expression and exchange, for instance on the Internet: they don't read *Le Monde Libertaire* or *Anarchist Studies*. And if they wish to hear our voice, we may try to participate in their discussions. They already have blogs, if they have access to computers.

4. It has about 2500 regular weekly sales (including subscriptions) and prints 8 to 10 thousand copies on particular occasions.

5. 'L'islamisme contre les femmes partout dans le monde'. See also, for instance, Marc Dupuy et Nicolas Truong, 'A Trappes, l'école coranique sème le trouble', *Le Monde de l'éducation*, n° 298, décembre 2001. There also was an aggression against five reporters who tried to film a Qur'anic school in a château in Grisy-Suisnes (Seine et Marne) on March 11, 2004.

6. Sharif Gemie mentions, for instance, 'Muslim scientific advances'.

7. See Eduardo Colombo, 'La religion et le pouvoir. Le sacré, l'apathie politique et l'hétéronomie,' *Réfractions* (Printemps 2005) n° 14, p. 5-16.

8. *L'Express*, 2 mai 2005, 'La face cachée de l'UOIF'.

9. We are discussing here existing state schools. What would be done in an anarchist education establishment would require another study.

10. This may be seen as a consequence of the revolutionary conception of the political sphere which rejects any consideration of people as *human beings*, with their different positions in society. Instead, it considers them as *abstract citizens* which, as such, are all equal. This Jacobinist metaphorical vision rejects all consideration of wealth, sex or opinion. Cf. also Marx's criticism, particularly in *On the Jewish*

question. A consequence of these principles is that all citizens can file a complaint if they feel that they are not treated as citizens but discriminated on account of their opinion, sex etc. This also implies that there cannot be any reverse discrimination.

11. On the contrary, the French political observer has seen on the left a clearly anticlerical (and anticommunist) party, the *radicaux-socialistes*, which now constitute the MRG (*Mouvement des radicaux de gauche*).

12. On this argument, see James C. Scott, *Seeing Like A State. How Certain Schemes to Improve the Human Condition Have Failed*. New Haven and London: Yale University, 1998.

13. This secret Catholic association has endeavoured to penetrate the various governments of the Republic, *Le Monde diplomatique*, September 1995, pp. 1, 22 and 23. The most notorious case was Michel Camdessus, former Governor of the Banque de France and from 1987 to 2000 director and chairman of the Executive Board of the International Monetary Fund. Camdessus was connected with Vatican Bank officials and with the Commission of Bishops within the European Union. See for instance, the editorial of *Europe Infos* (published by COMECE), n° 69 (mars 2005); Serge Halimi, 'Casse sociale sur fond de rapports officiels', *Le Monde diplomatique'*, Janvier 2005. Camdessus is now a member of the Pontifical Council on Justice and Peace which presents suggestions from the Holy See to the G8 meetings. He also has signed in the past a petition to include a reference to religion in the Charter of the European Union.

14. On January 2004 the group 'Aides' was condemned for 'public insults' to 'people because of their particular religion'. They had put out a poster with the words 'Holy Condom, protect us'; that condemnation was confirmed in April 2004 by the Upper Court in Toulouse. On March 2003 a poster representing da Vinci's Last Supper was prohibited because it represented women instead of Christ and the apostles.

15. See for instance J. Locke, *Lettre sur la tolérance*, Paris: PUF p. 83.

16. Catherine Kintzler, *La République en questions*, Minerve, 1996.

17. The estimation from the Haut Conseil à l'intégration is of 70,000. See: Délégation aux droits des femmes et à l'égalité des chances entre les hommes et les femmes, *Compte rendu* n° 11, Mardi 1 février 2005 (Séance de 18 heures).

18. Sondage IFOP, Octobre 2001.

19. Fides, Association 1901 (http://fides.ifrance.com/fides/html/islam1.html).

20. There is no excision in Algeria, Morocco or Tunisia. But if the Qur'an is totally silent on the subject, there is a *hadith* (tradition) reported by Abou Dâoûd, which mentions the practice with a recommendation from the prophet: 'not to operate too largely, it is better for the woman'. Excision antedates Islamism and is also practised by Christians in Eastern Africa in general. Cf. Leo Frobenius. *Kulturgeschichte Afrikas. Prologomena zu einer historischen Gestaltlehre*. Zürich: Phaidon Verlag, 1954. Reprint: Wuppertal: Peter Hammer Verlag, 1993, p.177.

21. The collège Gabriel-Havez at Creil, in the department of Oise. What triggered the issue was the fact that, in the last few years, Jewish pupils from the *Association de maison d'enfants* (AME) in the château de Laversine, near Creil, never came to school on Saturday mornings and, at the beginning of the school year, used to come ten days later than all the other children. In the June meeting of the school board (*conseil d'administration*), it was decided that no delay for religious reasons would be accepted at the next beginning of the school year. Other teachers then came to

talk of three young high school girls who wore the headscarf. If one asked the Jews to respect *laïcité* in school, one had to act in the same way for other religions. When the press brought to story in the news, they omitted to mention the fact that the event had been caused by the Jews. And it should be noted that the girls had identity photos without the veil. In other schools nearby, when the headscarf was accepted, the parents immediately asked that the girls be excused from certain courses, and so on. While in Creil the schoolgirls' position was at least ambiguous, elsewhere it appeared as religious.

22. As far as I know, the word 'Islamophobia' was created in Iran against Muslim women who refused to wear the veil. It was later used against Salman Rushdie. It was popularized in France by Tariq Ramadan.

23. There are Christian Arabs, for instance in Syria and Lebanon. The largest Muslim population is not Arab: it lives in Indonesia.

24. Alma and Lila LEVY, at the Lycée Henri-Wallon in Aubervilliers. Their version of the story is presented in Véronique Giraud, *Des filles comme les autres: Au-delà du foulard*(2004).

25. The father's position and explanation can be found at www.lmsi.net/article.php3?id_article=167.

26. Cf. the definition of these words in *Trésor de la langue française.*

27. The difference between the *hijab* and the headscarf is presented in Wikipedia: www.en.wikipedia.org/wiki/Hijab> and <http://en.wikipedia.org/wiki/Veil

28. www.endehors.org/news/4174.shtml.

29. Information directly obtained by Pierre Sommermeyer.

Afterword, but by no means the final word

L. SUSAN BROWN

Sharif Gemie is to be congratulated for broaching the thorny issue of the French government's banning of the headscarf in schools and for questioning the French anarchist position on the matter as represented in the pages of *Monde Libertaire*. The range of views Gemie's article has prompted in these pages is rich both in terms of style (from Beltrán Roca's academic prose to Tom Cahill's more conversational reflections) and content (from Harold B. Barclay's clear condemnation of the state's interference in the regulation of dress to Ronald Creagh's qualified support of a 'neutral public space' free of religious overtones). The diverse views are like succulent dishes brought to a pot luck, and fortunately for us, anarchists have no prohibition against discussing both politics and religion at the dinner table.

As I read through the collection of articles you have before you, a few questions came to mind. First is the question of when it is appropriate for the state to intervene in people's behaviour. Second is the specific French context of the debate, a context steeped in the struggle of the French state to limit the reach of the Catholic Church. And third is the issue of diversity itself.

When is it appropriate for the state to intervene in people's lives? As anarchists we properly reject the state as inherently oppressive. However, since we live in a world where the state is ubiquitous and not likely to wither away anytime soon, we may find ourselves at times supporting state action that is considered to be beneficial in some way or another. The anarchist position on religious headdress in French schools found in *Monde Libertaire* seems to me to take this position. State interference (a bad thing) is seen to be preferable over public religious expression (a worse thing). Others like Gemie argue that the new law prohibiting 'ostensible' religious symbols (like the Muslim scarf) is in effect 'the state's stigmatisation of a minority population' and not to be excused under any circumstances.

For me, a second and related issue – the importance of context – can help explain the different and sometimes even opposing positions on the French banning of the headscarf in schools. As Paul Chambers notes, 'clearly, context is everything'. The French context, with its Republican history of a 'neutral public realm' (*laïcité*) free of religious influence is one that is obviously important in this debate, but very difficult for those of us outside of France to comprehend fully. The fact that such a concept was used historically by the French state to limit the grip of the monolithic Catholic Church on its people is something that has great appeal to those of us who oppose the oppressiveness of institutionalized religion. France's very long and unique history of struggle between *the* church and *the* state has created an aura around this issue for the French. The applicability of this concept of *laïcité* today to areas in the world that are more culturally and religiously pluralistic, however, is not as obvious to those who stand outside the French context. Is the banning of religious headscarves in French schools truly preserving a neutral public realm, or is it doing just the opposite: subtly privileging the norms of the dominant Christian culture over those of the minority Muslim culture? Or is it simply an example of the modern state's propensity to micromanage people's lives for no logical reason other than because it can?

Finally, the last issue that this debate brought up for me is a topic that was only touched upon briefly in the articles – the positive value of diversity. Gemie alludes to this when he concludes that those who use the idea of *laïcité* to defend the banning of headscarves are basing their arguments on a universalism that 'never seems to consider whether there might be something to be learnt *from* other cultures.'

In some national and regional contexts, diversity is on the rise, and I firmly believe that diversity ought not to be just tolerated or merely managed, but wholeheartedly embraced and celebrated. Creativity, innovation and richness spring out of the mixing of difference. Nearly twenty-five years ago the social anarchist Murray Bookchin wrote about the possibility of grounding an anarchist ethics in nature, where 'nature is interpreted nonhierarchically, in terms of unity in diversity and spontaneity'.[1] More recently, and admittedly emerging out of an entirely different theoretical tradition, Richard Florida has taken this notion to the mainstream when he argues that economic prosperity in a capitalist context is correlated with several factors, including tolerance of difference. Creativity and innovation drive economic success, he argues, and creative and innovative people want to live in places that value diversity and are open to difference.

Regional economic growth is powered by creative people, who prefer places that are diverse, tolerant and open to new ideas. Diversity increases the odds that a place will attract different types of creative people with different skill sets and ideas. Places with diverse mixes of creative people are more likely to generate new combinations. Furthermore, diversity and concentration work together to speed the flow of knowledge. Greater and more diverse concentrations of creative capital in turn lead to higher rates of innovation, high-technology business formation, job generation and economic growth.[2]

While Florida's acceptance of capitalism sets him apart from most if not all anarchists, his observation about the positive value of diversity is very appealing and has merit in and of itself, independent of the specific economic system. All economies, whether they be capitalist, socialist or communist, benefit from the creativity and innovation that come about as a result of the interplay between diverse perspectives and ideas.

It is clear to me that how a country, or people or region approach the issue of diversity will have far-reaching consequences in this new, more interconnected, global world. Falling domestic birthrates combined with the wide adoption of free trade (involving not only the free movement of capital but the freer movement of people as well) means that the populations of many developed nations are undergoing a virtual demographic revolution. We no longer have the luxury of time to experiment with diversity; rather, for many countries, diversity is here to stay.

Again, context is everything. Take my home, Toronto, the largest city in Canada, as an example. With the exception of the First Nations People, Canada is a country of immigrants. Wave after wave of immigrants have settled here since even before Canada became a country. Statistics Canada, the country's government census bureau, tracks demographic information like country of origin, religion, language and other characteristics of our population. In 2001, Canada had a population of just under 30 million people. Out of that, 5.4 million, or 18.4% of the total population, were born outside the country. Only in Australia, where in 2001 22% of its population was foreign born, is the proportion of population born outside the country higher. In contrast, only 11% of the population of the United States was foreign born in 2000.[3]

The faces of immigrants to Canada have changed. Originally they were predominantly white from England and central Europe. Due to a shift in immigrant source countries, the visible minority population in Canada is growing much faster than the total population. Between 1996 and 2001, the total population increased 4% while the visible minority population rose 25% or six times faster.[4] This is reflected in Toronto, where the top ten countries of birth of immigrants in 2002 were India, China, Pakistan, Philippines, Iran, Sri Lanka, Korea, Russia, Ukraine and Jamaica.[5]

According to the 2001 census, Toronto attracted the largest share of new immigrants, nearly three times greater than its share of the total population of Canada. A total of 792,000 people who arrived in Canada during the 1990s were living in Toronto in 2001.[6] In 2001, the total population of the Toronto Census Metropolitan Area (CMA) was 4.6 million. The immigrant population was 2.0 million, or nearly 44%.

These simple facts – that 44% of Toronto's population are immigrants and that the visible/racial minority population is increasing six times faster than the total population – means that Toronto is undoubtedly one of the most racially and culturally diverse places on the planet. Close to 50% of Toronto's population are visible/racial minorities, and this is expected to increase to over 50% in the very near future. Immigrants come to Toronto from 172 countries of origin (for comparison, the United Nations has 190 member countries) and they speak over 100 different languages. Mass is said in 35 languages and 200,000 Muslims observe Ramadan. Over 80,000 Toronto Sikhs take part in annual Khalsa Day celebrations.

How is this diversity viewed in Canada and Toronto in particular? The state, both large and small, encourages diversity as a positive and essential value. The Canadian Charter of Rights and Freedoms contained in the Constitution Act of 1982 states: 'This Charter shall be interpreted in a manner consistent with the preservation and enhancement of the multicultural heritage of Canadians.'[7] In addition, the 1985 Canadian Multiculturalism Act affirms that it is 'the policy of the Government of Canada to recognize and promote the understanding that multiculturalism reflects the cultural and racial diversity of Canadian society and acknowledges the freedom of all members of Canadian society to preserve, enhance and share their cultural heritage'.[8]

On a more local level, the City of Toronto's official motto is 'Diversity Our Strength'. The City translates municipal election material into the top 16 languages by population in addition to English and French in order to encourage voter participation: Arabic, Chinese, Greek, Italian, Korean, Farsi, Polish, Portuguese, Punjabi, Russian, Spanish, Tagalog, Tamil, Ukrainian, Urdu and Vietnamese. Toronto Public Health delivers services in 30 languages. The Toronto Public Library loans over 4 million items in languages other than English. Street signs in Chinatown are bilingual (English/Chinese), as they are in other ethnic-oriented Toronto neighbourhoods like Greektown and Little India.

Expressions of diverse religious observance are part of everyday life in Canada. Sikhs serving with the Toronto police force are permitted to wear turbans while on duty, as are those who serve with the Royal Canadian Mounted Police (RCMP). Prayer rooms are made available to Muslim employees of the City of Toronto. In order to serve the widest possible population, women and girls in Toronto are offered separate women-only swim times in publicly funded pools that include women-only instruction, with specific outreach to the Muslim community.

This acknowledgement of multiculturalism as a fact of life transcends state institutions and is part of Toronto's business and cultural ethos. Last week I used a bank machine at one of Canada's top banks that was located in Chinatown and I was given the option of selecting Chinese as the language in which to make my transaction. Toronto is home to 110 ethnic business associations, from the Belgian Canadian Business Association to the Vietnamese Business and Professional Club. Estimates of the number of ethnic publications based in Toronto vary from 100 to as high as 300, including daily newspapers in Chinese, Italian, Spanish and Korean.[9] Delicacies the world over are served in Toronto restaurants that range from Ethiopian to South Indian cuisine and everything in between.

Of course this path of diversity is not without its bumps. It is taking longer now than it did twenty years ago for new immigrants to catch up economically with their Canadian-born counterparts.[10] While the Canadian immigration system is selecting for those who are highly skilled and educated (the average immigrant arriving today has more education than the average native-born Canadian), our professional regulatory bodies and businesses are slow to recognize immigrants' skills, experience and credentials. There is much concerted effort being expended by social service agencies, pubic policy groups, governments and immigrants themselves to shift attitudes and behaviours, and changes are slowly being made.[11] But we are at least starting from a place where multiculturalism is not feared but welcomed. A recent survey in the Greater Toronto Area (GTA) asked residents if they thought the number of immigrants into Canada should be increased, decreased or remain the same. The response was positive – 49 per cent of respondents felt that immigration levels should remain the same, and 16 per cent answered that numbers should be increased. Further to this, 68 per cent agreed that Canada should take responsibility to provide opportunities for skilled immigrants after they have arrived in Canada.[12]

In Canada, then, it is clear that there is both popular and political support for a multicultural society where large numbers of newcomers are welcomed on an ongoing basis. Cahill suggests that the French tend to regard multiculturalism as a flawed and unsuccessful Anglo-Saxon model. The pluralism of today is something that the French have a hard time making sense of, coming as they do from a history where a monolithic state stood against a monolithic church.

The political philosopher Bhikhu Parekh defends multiculturalism from its detractors, arguing that it provides us with three important and complementary insights: 'the cultural embeddedness of human beings, the inescapability and desirability of cultural plurality, and the plural and multicultural nature of each culture.' He goes on to state:

> When we view the world from its [a multiculturalist] vantage point, our attitudes to ourselves and others undergo profound changes. All claims that a particular institution or way of thinking or living is perfect, the best, or necessitated by human nature itself appear incoherent and even bizarre, for it goes against our well-considered conviction that all ways of thought and life are inherently limited and cannot embody the full range of the richness, complexity and grandeur of human existence.[13]

Speaking at Metropolis, an international conference on immigration held in Toronto in October 2005, Parekh spoke passionately about the need to understand cultural diversity as both a fact and a value, and suggested that it is in intercultural dialogue that we can find balance. He argued against '*multi*-culturalism', a sort of cultural relativism where separate cultures are all equal, and in favour of '*multicultural*-ism', where the interconnectedness and intercommunication of cultures are encouraged to thrive.

It is in this context – and remember, context is everything – that I considered the issue of the veil. In Toronto, whether in schools, in the street, in shopping malls, in restaurants, on subways or buses, or in squares, parks and other public spaces, it is not uncommon to see observant Jews wearing yarmulkes, Sikhs wearing turbans, Hindu women wearing saris with bindis painted on their foreheads, Falun Gong practitioners performing their exercises, Rastafarians with their hair in dreadlocks, and Buddhist monks in their saffron-coloured robes. It is in this atmosphere that Muslim women and girls of all ages are routinely seen in public – including schools – sometimes partially covered, sometimes with their bodies fully draped. While I personally question the liberatory nature of the veil when it is so complete as to leave the wearer entirely hidden, I live with my discomfort because, from the outside, I cannot know what it means to the woman herself, and I do not believe I have the right to judge her. Instead, I accept her difference and feel proud that I live in a pluralistic place where we can all be different yet live together in relative peace. In what sort of place do you want to live?

Toronto, January 2006

I would like to thank Thomas S. Martin, Randy McLean and Steve Karpik for reviewing initial drafts of this paper and providing valuable suggestions and comments.

NOTES

1. Murray Bookchin, *The Ecology of Freedom* (Cheshire Books: Palo Alto, 1982), p. 274.

2. Richard Florida, *The Rise of the Creative Class* (Perseus Books: New York, 2003), p. 249.

3. *2001 Census: Analysis Series, Canada's Ethnocultural Portrait: The Changing Mosaic* (Statistics Canada, 2003), p. 5.

4. *Population Projections of Visible Minority Groups, Canada, Provinces and Regions, 2001 to 2017* (Statistics Canada, March 2005).

5. *Toronto Business and Market Guide 2004: A Profile of the Toronto Region* (Toronto: The Toronto Board of Trade, 2004), p. 170.

6. *2001 Census: Analysis Series, Canada's Ethnocultural Portrait: The Changing Mosaic* (Statistics Canada, 2003), p. 7.

7. The Canadian Charter of Rights and Freedoms, The Constitution Act, 1982 (laws.justice.gc.ca/en/const/index.html).

8. Canadian Multiculturalism Act, 1985 (laws.justice.gc.ca/en/C-18.7/index.html).

9. *Toronto Business and Market Guide 2004: A Profile of the Toronto Region* (Toronto: The Toronto Board of Trade, 2004), p. 40-41.

10. See *Explaining the Deteriorating Entry Earnings of Canada's Immigrant Cohorts: 1966-2000* (Statistics Canada, May 2004); and 'The Discounting of Immigrants' Skills in Canada: Evidence and Policy Recommendations', by Naomi Alboim, Ross Finnie and Ronald Meng, *IRPP Choices*, Vol. 11, No. 2, February 2005.

11. For example, 'Tapping Immigrants' Skills: New Directions for Canadian Immigration Policy in the Knowledge Economy', by Jeffery G. Reitz, *IRPP Choices*, Vol. 11, No. 1, February 2005. See also the Toronto Region Immigrant Employment Council at www.triec.ca.

12. 'Immigration Works: The GTA Weighs in on Skilled Immigrants and the Workforce', Toronto Region Immigrant Employment Council, June 2004, p. 1.

13. 'What is Multiculturalism', by Bhikhu Parekh, in *Multiculturalism: A Symposium on Democracy in Culturally Diverse Societies*, #484, December 1999 (www.india-seminar.com/1999/484/484%20parekh.htm).

Research Note: Αναρχία – What did the Greeks actually say?

URI GORDON

Doctoral Candidate in Politics
University of Oxford
uri.gordon@mansf.ox.ac.uk

ABSTRACT

This article examines a range of uses to which the word 'anarchy' and its derivations were put in ancient Greek sources. Perhaps not surprisingly, the majority of instances indicate that the negative application of the word as a synonym for confusion and disorder was prevalent from ancient times. However, there are also several eminently political uses, which are quite telling in their prefiguration of contemporary anarchist values – namely the Athenians' reference to 404 BC as the 'year of anarchy'; the uses of the word by Plato and Aristotle in their critiques of democracy; and the association of anarchy with the defiant actions of Antigone in the plays of Aeschylus and Sophocles.

The ancient Greek origin of the word 'anarchy' is a matter of common knowledge, and it has become a predictable convention to mention it at the outset of almost any discussion of anarchism as a political movement in the modern era. At the same time, as far as I am aware, no one has ever looked at the actual functioning of the word in classical sources. Instead, anarchist and non-anarchist commentators alike have inevitably satisfied themselves with second-hand exercises in Greek etymology, removing the word from its discursive context and ignoring the complex array of meanings it had for ancient writers. What I propose here, then, is to give attention to the actual uses to which the word was put in classical Greek. As I think will become immediately clear, such an exercise is of more than a merely historical interest.

Greek political culture revolved around citizenship in the *polis*, the city-state form that dominated political organization in the Hellenic world form the archaic period (c.800 BC) to the strong-armed unification of Greece under Alexander the Great (356-323 BC). Due in part to the penin-sula's geographic conditions, which meant that many settlement-clusters developed in relative isolation, *poleis* bringing together hundreds of farming households were largely self-sufficient and enjoyed economic and

84

political autonomy for centuries. The typical Greek *polis* was a complex hierarchical society, with chattel slavery in agricultural households serving as its economic base. Sharply separated from domestic life was the citizen body, in which a certain rough equality obtained among male property owners. Citizenship was not necessarily 'democratic' – in Sparta, all soldiers/citizens belonged to an assembly that elected a ruling council, which had legislative authority and advised the King. But in whatever form, the ideal of citizenship in a united political community seems to have been universally accepted by all literate classes. The *polis* itself was a matter for collective pride and was valued beyond question as the hallmark of the superiority of Greek civilization to the lifestyles of surrounding 'barbarian' tribes. (See the bibliography for some further reading on the history and character of Greek political societies.)

Given the pervasive currency of this worldview, it is perhaps not surprising that, as T. A. Sinclair notes, 'there was no philosophy of anarchy in Greek political theory'.[1] There are some possible exceptions to this observation: there were Cynics such as Antisthenes (a pupil of Socrates, c.444-365 BC) and his own pupil Diogenes of Sinope (412-323 BC), who looked with disdain on conventional values, wealth and social status, and who would have seen government as opposed to a life in full accordance with nature. Unfortunately only small fragments of Cynic writings have survived, but their ideas are thought to have later influenced Zeno of Citium (333-264 BC), founder of Stoicism, 'who distinctly opposed his conception of a free community without government to the state-utopia of Plato ... repudiated the omnipotence of the state, its intervention and regimentation, and proclaimed the sovereignty of the moral law of the individual'.[2] However, the Cynics' purism drove them to oppose any organised intervention in politics, making their 'anarchism' philosophical at best. While the ease with which later developments in Stoicism were appropriated for the peace of mind of the Roman emperor Marcus Aurelius (121-180 AD) shows that its anarchist resonances were neither obvious nor perennial. Finally, neither Cynics nor Stoics are known to have used the actual concept 'anarchy'.

Surprisingly, the entire corpus of electronically surveyable literature in ancient Greek contains only 47 instances of the word '*anarkhia*' or its derivations.[3] Compared to 549 instances of '*demokratia*' and 422 of '*oligarkhia*' in the same database, the word does not seem to have occupied a significant place in the literary vocabulary of the time. Among these 47 instances, moreover, the majority of cases employ the word just as many non-anarchists might do today – as a catch-all synonym for confusion, disorder, tumult and license. Thus in the play *Hecuba* by Euripides (c.480-406 BC), the heroine, fearing for her daughter's body, says that 'the mob knows no restraint, and the unruliness [*anarkhia*] of sailors exceeds

85

that of fire'.[4] Another playwright, Aeschylus (c.525-456 BC), has his Clytaemnestra (wife of king Agamemnon, who fought against Troy) recalling the warning that 'the mob's anarchic will [*dêmothrous anarkhia*] might overturn the Council'.[5] While the historian Thucydides (c.460-395 BC) attributes the military failures of the Syracusans in part to 'the troops' disorder [*asyntakton anarkhian*]'.[6] The same type of usage is also found in the historical work of Herodotus (c.484-430 BC), as well as with later Greek-writing historians such as Diodorus Siculus (fl.50 AD) and Flavius Josephus (c.37-100 AD). We can thus see that, far from being a subsequent 'corruption', the negative and condemnatory connotations of the word anarchy have burdened it from earliest times.

Let us look, however, at other cases from ancient Greece in which the word anarchy is used in a more distinctly political sense. There is, for instance, the single occasion when a Hellenic population appears to have matter-of-factly used the word to refer to its own situation: the Athenian 'year of anarchy', 404 BC. This is something of a curiosity, since the circumstances of that year were anything but anarchic. As a matter of fact, Athens was at the time under the very strong rule of an oligarchy – The Thirty – installed by the Spartans following their victory in the second Peloponesian war of that same year. Moreover, there was literally an *Archon* in place, installed by the oligarchs, in the person of Pythodorus. However, according to the historian Xenophon (c.430-355 BC), the Athenians refused to apply here their custom of calling the year by that archon's name, since he was elected during the oligarchy, and 'preferred to speak of it as the "year of anarchy"'.[7] Despite its counter-intuitive appearance, this first popular application of the word anarchy is very telling. It resonates with a mass symbolic defiance, refusing the recognition that a ruler was supposed to receive in everyday language. It was this defiance which led to the restoration of democracy in Athens the following year.

Democracy, of course, was far from a positive ideal for the great political theorists of ancient Greece, Plato and Aristotle. And it was always in the context of discussing democracy that they made their rare uses of the word anarchy – making for the close association between the two concepts which would prevail well into the modern era.[8] The two philosophers' famous mistrust of democracy, rooted in their contempt for popular power of any kind, was expressed in their arguments for democracy's inherent vulnerability and its preponderance to deteriorate into tyranny. However, it should be noticed that what enabled Plato to present such arguments in the *Republic* was the complete detachment of his account of democracy from the realities of such systems of government, in Athens and elsewhere. Nowhere does his description reflect the constitution that sentenced his mentor Socrates to death, the structured, lawful and impeccably stratified Hellenic democracy. Instead, we find an account that comes very close to what we might intuitively call anarchy, though for Plato this is an entirely negative affair. In democracy, he says, there is no enforceable political authority or stability of the state, 'no necessity ... for you to govern ... even if you have the capacity, or to be governed, unless you like, or to go to war when the rest go to war, or to be at peace when others are at peace, unless you are so disposed'.⁹ This portrayal is what sets the ground for Plato's account of such a state's subsequent deterioration into tyranny. Democracy in his view makes for far too much equality. It loosens what Plato considered to be the natural hierarchy and authority obtaining between slave and master, man and woman, parent and child. His allegorical youngster's soul, divided between an oligarchical self and a democratic self, is besieged by the corrupting and evil influence of the latter. Democracy causes the soul to 'drink too deeply from the strong wine of freedom', breeding desires whose false councils introduce 'insolence and anarchy and waste and impudence ... hymning their praises and calling them by sweet names; insolence they term breeding, and anarchy liberty [anarkhian de eleutherian], and waste magnificence, and impudence courage'. So pervasive is the corruption that 'anarchy finds a way into the private houses, and ends by getting among the animals and infecting them'.¹⁰ In order to avoid the dangers of anarchy, Plato concludes that habits of dominance and obedience must be instilled deeply into the soul of the individual. 'This task of ruling, and being ruled by, others must be practised in peace from earliest childhood; but anarchy must be utterly removed from the lives of all mankind, and of the beasts also that are subject to man'.¹¹

It is important to note that, for Plato, anarchy is never a distinct class of political association. Since the concept is entirely subsumed into his discussion of democracy, it is not understood as requiring a separate theoretical category alongside oligarchy, tyranny, democracy, etc. Nevertheless, Plato's account does supply us with an important understanding about anarchy that remains intact regardless of his crusade against it. This is that anarchy represents not merely the lack of government conceived as statelessness, but also the thorough erosion of rank in non-governmental spheres – between classes, age-groups and genders.

Aristotle's association of anarchy with democracy is essentially identical to Plato's, although his depiction thereof is never as colourful. The concept appears again as a form of democratic deterioration, but in keeping with Aristotle's method it is appropriately situated in empirical observations rather than in metaphorical speculation. In democracies such as Thebes and Syracuse, we are told, the upper classes were motivated to stage a coup by their contempt for the prevailing 'disorder and anarchy [ataxias kai anarkhias]' in the affairs of the state.¹² Also, in many cases the nobles will form factions with one another, and create them among the masses, 'and so bring about a suspension of government [anarkhian]'.¹³

Alternately, in a tyranny Aristotle sees 'democratic' features, namely 'license among slaves' [*anarkhia te doulôn*] as well as among women and children. 'A constitution of this sort', he concludes, 'will have a large number of supporters, as disorderly living [*zên ataktôs*] is pleasanter to the masses than sober living'.[14] Aristotle, like Plato, was not interested in delineating anarchy as a separate political form. However, unlike Plato, he is able to see anarchy as more than an abstractly corrupting influence, since its connection with democracy portrays it as desirable by the masses, and even as an implicit goal of popular insurrection.

The explicit connection of anarchy with a conscious human will appears only twice in classical Greek literature. This is perhaps the most intriguing example since, although penned by two different authors over a gap of several decades, they both refer to the same act by the same person. If we are looking for the first-ever anarchist, here she is:

> **Antigone:** I at least will say something to the rulers of the Cadmeans: even if no one else is willing to share in burying him I will bury him alone and risk the peril of burying my own brother. Nor am I ashamed to act in defiant opposition [*apiston tênd' anarkhian*] to the rulers of the city. A thing to be held in awe is the common womb from which we were born, of a wretched mother and unfortunate father. Therefore, my soul, willingly share his evils, even though they are unwilling, and live in kindred spirit with the dead. No hollow-bellied wolves will tear his flesh, let no one 'decree' that! Even though I am a woman, I will myself find the means to give him burial and a grave, carrying the earth in the fold of my linen robe. With my own hands I will cover him over – let no one 'decree' it otherwise. Take heart, I will have the means to do it.[15]

In the person of Antigone, a long-standing inspiration to feminists, we also find a clear prefiguration of two of the most important concepts attached to anarchist practice in its contemporary idiom: disobedience and direct action. First, Antigone openly refuses to abide by the rulers' decree to leave her brother Polyneices' body unburied, as punishment for his participation in the attack on Thebes. She asserts that the bond of siblings born of a common womb stands above the authority of political powers, and rejects the legitimacy of any decree that transgresses this bond. While her appeal to values that stand above the law as a justification for her actions is by no means an exclusively anarchist refrain, and while on some interpretations these values are themselves grounded in a form of authority – the higher authority of the gods – it is the disobedient and insubordinate character of her action that she, in her own words, associates with anarchy. It should also be remembered that it was only in recent decades that the notion of justified, 'civil' disobedience to the law acquired popular moral legitimacy. In earlier times, including those of the anarchist movement in the nineteenth and early twentieth centuries, the distinction between contingent and wholesale (i.e. anarchist) rejection of political authority was not as clear as it is today.

Second, we find in Antigone's speech a striking example of the concept of direct action. She has no intention of appealing to the authorities in order to convince them of the immorality or illegitimacy of their decree, but rather takes that illegitimacy as her starting point, and sets about to take matters into her own hands and create by herself the alternate reality that she desires. Aeschylus, we may also note, has his chorus openly endorse Antigone's defiance at the close of the play. Whatever action the authorities might take against her, they say, 'We, at all events, will go and bury him with her, following the funeral procession. For this grief is shared by all our race, and the city approves, as just, different things at different times'.[16]

Picking up the narrative in *Antigone*, Sophocles has the autocrat Creon warn his son Heimon (who is also Antigone's lover) of the dangers of her intended action:

Creon: There is no evil worse than disobedience [*anarkhias de meizon ouk estin kakon*]. This destroys cities; this overturns homes; this breaks the ranks of allied spears into headlong rout. But the lives of men who prosper upright, of these obedience has saved the greatest part. Therefore we must defend those who respect order, and in no way can we let a woman defeat us.[17]

Again the translator has well chosen to reflect the disobedient core of anarchy, whereas Sophocles himself cleverly exposes here the ambiguity and half-heartedenss of all rulers' moralistic declamations in defence of obedience and authority. Is the issue here really the potential damage to the collectivity of such an act of disobedience going unpunished? Or is it rather the danger that such an example of defiance would posit to the stability of power itself and, even more poignantly, to the principle of male supremacy?

To be sure, neither the classical Greek nor any other historical antecedents of the uses of the word anarchy should have any deciding influence on how we might understand the concept today. However, the foregoing analysis of the ancient literature does lead to two significant conclusions about the discourse surrounding the word. First, we can see that the negative connotations of anarchy with disorder and confusion have been widespread from the very beginning, as evident in the first citations I offered. This shows how deep-seated are the preconceptions which anarchists have had to deal with when re-articulating the word as a positive ideal. Second, we can see that despite these widespread connotations, some writers *were* capable of understanding anarchy as an eminently political concept – even if it had an entirely negative role in their writing. Moreover, these political formulations of anarchy already contain, in their most ancient form, the notions of social equality, popular resistance and disobedience to power which anarchists associate with their project to this day.

Acknowledgements: My thanks to Dimitrios Kyritsis and Juan Coderch for verifying Greek translations.

NOTES

1. Sinclair (1951:83).
2. Kropotkin (1910), Marshall (1992:68-71).
3. The figures here are taken from the comprehensive database of the *Perseus Digital Library* at Tufts University. See .
4. Euripides, *Hecuba* ll.606-8.
5. Thucydides, *The Peloponesian War*, bk.6 ch.72 §4.
6. Aeschylus, *Agamemnon*, ll.883-4.
7. Xenophon, *Hellenica*, bk.2 ch.3 §1.
8. Before Pierre Joseph Proudhon became the first to use the word in a positive sense in 1840, 'anarchists' was a widespread pejorative for 'democrats'. See Williams (1976:37-8).
9. Plato, *Republic*, bk.8.
10. Ibid.
11. Plato, *Laws* §942c. Note that here as in the previous citation, Plato seems to be hinting at a continuity between hierarchy among humans and the domesticated state of non-human animals, with anarchy corrupting both. One wonders whether our contemporary anarcho-primitivists would appreciate such a strange bedfellow …
12. Aristotle, *Politics*, bk.5 ch.3.
13. *op.cit.*, bk.2 ch.10.
14. *op.cit.*, bk.6 ch.4.
15. Aeschylus, *Seven Against Thebes*, ll.1032-1045. Dated at 467 BC, this also happens to be the earliest recorded use of the a-word.
16. Ibid., ll.1074-1077.
17. Sophocles, *Antigone*, ll.672-678.

BIBLIOGRAPHY

1. Works cited
Aeschylus 1926. *Aeschylus* (trans. H. W. Smyth). Cambridge, MA, Harvard University Press.
Aristotle 1932. *Politics* (trans. H. Rackham). Cambridge, MA, Harvard University Press.

Ἀναρχία – WHAT DID THE GREEKS ACTUALLY SAY?

Euripides 1938. *Hecuba* (trans. E. P. Coleridge). New York, Random House.
Kropotkin, P. 1910. 'Anarchism', *Encyclopaedia Britannica* article.
Marshall, P. 1993. *Demanding the Impossible: a history of anarchism.* London, Fontana.
Plato 1901. Republic (trans. B. Jowett). New York, P. F. Collier.
Plato 1926. *Laws* (trans. R.G. Bury). New York, Putnam.
Sinclair, T. A. 1951. *A History of Greek Political Thought.* London, Routledge & Kegan Paul.
Sophocles 1891. *Antigone* (trans. R. Jebb). Cambridge, Cambridge University Press.
Thucydides 1910. *The Peloponnesian War* (trans. R. Crawley). London, Dent.
Williams, Raymond 1976. 'Anarchism', *Keywords.* London, Fontana.
Xenophon 1985. *Hellenica* (trans. C.L. Brownson). Cambridge, MA, Harvard University Press.

2. Background on ancient Greek politics

Andrewes, A. 1971. *Greek Society.* Harmondsworth, Penguin.
Baslez, M. F. 1994. *Histoire politique du monde grec antique.* Paris, Nathan.
Brock, R. and S. Hodkinson (eds.) 2000. *Alternatives to Athens: varieties of political organization. and community in ancient Greece.* Oxford, Oxford University Press.
Meier, C.1990. *The Greek discovery of politics.* Cambridge, MA, Harvard University Press.
Nielsen, T. H. (ed.) 2004. *Once again: studies in the ancient Greek Polis.* Stuttgart, Franz Steiner.
Rhodes, P. (ed.) 2004. *Athenian democracy.* Edinburgh, Edinburgh University Press.
Sinclair, R. K. 1988. *Democracy and participation in Athens.* Cambridge, Cambridge University Press.
Starr, Chester G. 1986. *Individual and community: the rise of the* polis. Oxford, Oxford University Press.

The Divided Forecast for Academic Anarchism in America

SPENCER SUNSHINE

It's an interesting time for anarchists in the academy in the US. On one hand, we are now six years after the Seattle demonstrations. Many anti-globalization movement activists have entered graduate programs and are creating a renaissance in anarchist studies. Their interests range the whole gamut of radical theorizing, and a variety of groups and conferences are emanating from this. A flush of serious works are being published about anarchism, the likes of which hasn't been seen since the collapse of the 'classical' movement.

On the other hand, in the States at least, things have not been so grim for radicals in the university system since the McCarthyism of the 1950s, although it has not sunk to the same depth (yet?). Rightists such as David Horowitz and misnamed groups like Students for Academic Freedom seek to cleanse the universities of radicals. It was only after the 1960s that Marxism took hold in the US academy. Instinctively, its practitioners took to mole behaviour and carved deep niches in the university system – after all, Marxism never met a bureaucracy it didn't love. The Marxists' academic entrenchment gave them a solid base of support. Not just do they (like all academic currents) have a tendency to hire their own kind, but also they provide mutual defence against common enemies.

However, anarchists and other non-Marxist radicals have no such support system. While the overwhelming zeitgeist of the 1960s had been anarchist, the energy was largely channelled into Third Worldist Leninism or apolitical cultural and spiritual trends, and only a tiny number of anarchists became academics. In fact, the most prominent US anarchist academics of the last few decades – Noam Chomsky, Paul Avrich and Murray Bookchin – all hailed from earlier generations.

The cases of David Graeber and Ward Churchill illustrate the current predicaments of non-Marxist radical academics. In February of 2004, well-known Native American radical scholar and American Indian Movement activist Churchill came under intense national scrutiny for an essay he published. (Churchill is also an anarchist-sympathizer with books on AK Press.) 'Some People Push Back: On the Justice of Roosting Chickens' said what many people thought but didn't dare say out loud: that the 11 September massacre was a response to US imperialism. But Churchill's incendiary tone (and some out-of-context quotes) made him vulnerable. The media outcry included two state governors essentially labelling him a 'terrorist'. The pressure forced him to step down from his position as department chair but he refused to resign. He was protected by the still-existent tenure system, which – at its best – exists for exactly this kind of incidence: to protect professors who make politically unpopular statements. (It was soon revealed that the Colorado governor was making a case of Churchill as part of a larger plan to remove tenure altogether from the state schools.) Currently he is still hanging tough and retains his position.

David Graeber presents another case altogether. In the super-hierarchical academic system, he is easily one of the highest-placed anarchists – although this will soon be past tense, as he recently failed to pass what is generally accepted as a rubber-stamp department renewal last year. No official reasons were given (in fact the whole process is secret) but wide-spread speculation points to his (mis) identification in the media as an anarchist spokesperson during the 2002 anti-World Economic Forum protests in New York City. Or the attempt by right-wing Yale alumni to have him removed afterwards. Or his defence of a department grad student who was engaged in a hotly-contested union organizing drive.

Graeber was dismissed a couple years before he would be eligible for tenure, at which point one would reasonably expect not to have their contract renewed. If academics are able to get to the point where they come up for tenure (the year before they complete ten years of teaching), they have a 12-20% chance of getting it. Graeber was initially hired for three years; went through a review for the next three years; and towards the end of the next four-year cycle would have been up for tenure. But after his first three-year renewal he started engaging in public activist work. This resulted in his identification as an anarchist in the mass media, which resulted in the campaign to have him removed. Initially, something happened in the (secret) review for the next four years. It went to a dean, who ruled that his contract be extended for two years, instead of four, and then reviewed for the last two. Graeber's dismissal came at this point, and he is now finishing his eighth year of teaching.

A large outcry followed; his students mobilized in his defence and their online petition has been signed by over 4,500 people. A bill was even introduced in the EU parliament in support of him. He contested the firing, and in December 2005 he accepted an agreement whereby he was paid off with a one-year sabbatical if he dropped his appeal and agreed not to return. The anarchist response has been interesting: while there has been a fair amount of support, others have made comments like 'Fuck you, serves you right for selling out to the man!' Even if we put aside the question of whether teaching in the university consists of 'selling-out', Graeber's situation (after all, nobody doubts that he can land another job) seems far less worthy of support than, say, jailed anarchists or activists framed by the FBI.

But there are larger issues here that could potentially affect everyone – not to mention what's just plumb fucked-up about any radical losing their job on the basis of their politics. Higher education is practically the only major sector in our society where radicals have established a serious foothold and can function openly. If a precedent is set for purging radicals in the universities, this could easily open the door to this occurring at all levels in society.

In lieu of a fundamental transformation of the economic and social relationships of our society, we are all dependent on the present system to get by. (Even squatters, dumpster-divers and train-hoppers are dependent on capitalism to overproduce goods which can be occupied, scavenged or boarded.) If the Right can dislodge radicals in one of our only strongholds, it will have cleared any potential obstacles to sweeping us out of all the workplaces where we are forced to toil.

Graeber's dismissal comes at a particularly interesting moment in the relationship between anarchism and the academy. Just as the grad students are banging on the door to get in, one of the most prominent of the very few professors already in the system is being booted out. What this means for the future of anarchists in academia, at least in America, remains to be seen.

Announcing the establishment of a
Political Science Association (UK) Specialist Study Group:

Specialist Group for the Study of Anarchism

Department of Politics, IR and European Studies (PIRES),
Loughborough University, UK.

In the wake of renewed interest in anarchist thought, the PSA *Specialist Group for the Study of Anarchism* (SGSA) will facilitate and promote the academic study of anarchism. This will be done by providing an institutional forum to bring graduate students, activists and professional academics together, to share the latest research and developments in anarchist theory and practice. The specialist working group will also provide an interdisciplinary platform through which anarchism can be promoted as a viable practical, conceptual, and pedagogical paradigm for 21st century academia. PSA study groups are eligible for up to £1,500 per annum to fund their activities. One of the primary aims of the group is to use official PSA recognition as a platform for further research funding applications.

Other proposed projects of the working group include the following:

1. The organisation of a biannual seminar series for graduate students.
2. The organisation of an annual two-day conference on the legacy and work of individual anarchists or aspects of anarchist history, contemporary anarchist practice, or anarchism's potential to contribute (analytically/pragmatically) to political and economic change.
3. An annual public lecture by leading anarchist academics/activists.
4. Coordinating publication strategies. This will include publication in the refereed journal *Anarchist Studies*, and liaison with other publishers and on-line magazines, as well as publication in more generic political science journals.
5. Coordinating broader and long-term research projects.
6. Facilitate engagement and mutual learning between anarchist academic and activist groups.

**SGSA membership is free, so please encourage as many
people to join as possible!!**

If you would like to join the group, have any suggestions for future activities, or would like any further information, please contact:

Alex Prichard (SGSA Secretary) at: a.prichard@lboro.ac.uk

Instructions for authors

Contributions will be considered on the condition that they are not currently under consideration for publication elsewhere. Papers can be in English, French, Spanish or German. However, authors of non-English language papers may be asked to supply a draft translation into English *before* any final decision to publish is made.

All papers considered for publication will be sent to three readers. Four copies should be supplied, typed and double-spaced, paginated, and on A4 paper. The first page should list the author's name, the title of the paper, and a postal and e-mail address. The second page should begin with the title of the paper. No indication of author's identity should be given in the rest of the paper. Authors whose papers are accepted will be asked to supply an electronic copy of their paper.

Authors may make use of any recognised academic reference system, as long as it is clear and used coherently. Authors should avoid using specialist jargon and acronyms. Papers should be between 5,000 and 12,000 words long. The editors reserve the right to make alterations which do not involve a change of meaning.

Papers accepted become copyright of the journal unless specifically agreed to the contrary: contributors are free to re-use material after publication in not-for-profit publications, provided that *Anarchist Studies* is clearly acknowledged as the original place of publication. Commercial publishers who wish to re-publish papers should contact the publishers of *Anarchist Studies* in order to negotiate terms.

Contributions and further questions should be sent to the editor:

Dr S. Gemie, Humanities, University of Glamorgan, Pontypridd, CF37 1DL, UK. (sgemie@glam.ac.uk)